CELEBRATION OF
VICTORY

V-E DAY 1945

Richard Connaughton voluntarily ended his Army career as Head of the British Army's Defence Studies. His specialism was transportation but he also spent seven years seconded to the Brigade of Gurkhas and was a member of staff at both the British and Australian Army Staff Colleges. He now spends his time divided equally between conducting specialist studies for clients and writing books which interest him.

Richard Connaughton is author of *Shrouded Secrets: Japan's War on Mainland Australia 1942–44*, also published by Brassey's.

Richard Connaughton

CELEBRATION OF VICTORY

VICTORY

V-E DAY 1945

BRASSEY'S
LONDON • WASHINGTON

Copyright © 1995 Brassey's (UK) Ltd

First English Edition 1995

UK editorial offices: Brassey's, 33 John Street, London WC1N 2AT
UK orders: Marston Book Services, PO Box 87, Oxford OX2 0DT

North American Orders: Brassey's Inc., PO Box 960, Herndon, VA 22070

Richard Connaughton has asserted his moral right to be
identified as the author of this work.

Library of Congress Cataloging in Publication Data
available

British Library Cataloguing in Publication Data
A catalogue record for this book is available from the British Library

ISBN 1 85753 181 7 Flexicover

Typeset by M Rules
Printed in Great Britain by The Bath Press, Bath

For those who were there

ACKNOWLEDGEMENTS

The author wishes to thank the Secretary General and Staff of The Royal British Legion and the Director General and Staff of The Imperial War Museum for their assistance in the compilation of this book. The photographs have been taken from the archives of The Imperial War Museum except where attributed separately.

The author also thanks all those who have contributed to this book either directly themselves or by way of Executors and Trustees. The author is grateful for the opportunity to quote from Norman Gelb's *Scramble. A Narrative History of the Battle of Britain;* Jonathan Croall's *Don't You Know There's a War on? – The People's Voice 1939–1945*, the *Hampshire Magazine*, and Mollie Panter Downes' *London War Notes 1939–1945*. Thanks are also due to Dorset County Museum, William Crutchley, Jack Norman, Sybil McLaughlin, Tony Trythall and Eric Grove. Finally to ARGC for patience, the usual blend of skill, forbearance and advice – solicited or otherwise.

CONTENTS

Acknowledgements 6

Introduction 9

Causes, Preparation and the Beginning of War 11

Bearing the Strain 41

The Home Front 68

Celebration of Victory 100

Postscript: Three Peers, the War and Peace 146

INTRODUCTION

W hen to celebrate, when to commemorate, that is the question. It was a compelling question raised at the 50th anniversary of the D-Day landings. Since the invasion of Europe was the commencement of a continuing military action, it was arguably more appropriate to mark the event by way of a commemoration and leave the celebration until war in Europe had finally come to an end. This subtle difference between commemoration and celebration was lost in what became a political furore, seemingly lacking nothing but consultation with the interested parties. This book most emphatically concerns the celebration of Victory in Europe, or V-E Day, on 8 May 1945.

As circumstances would show, the celebration of this victory was rather more than bonfires, street parties, a day of dancing and the opportunity to kiss strangers. The victory had been anticipated and, to some degree, it was anti-climactic. There were also those who had relatives being reorganised to take the fight on to Japan. Setting all that aside, V-E Day was an important marker in the nation's political, social and military history. It seemed to promise to the nation's disadvantaged a more equitable share in the life, the wealth and the decision-making processes in a re-born country.

Two nations went to war but they won that war as one. The greatest bonding had occurred in the middle order. Conscripts in the emergent Citizens' Army were subjected to a subtle, socialist propaganda campaign which spanned the entire war and went uncontested. While the people had great confidence in Winston Churchill as a war leader, a majority did not see him as a convincing peacetime leader of a party so closely associated with their own domestic ills and with appeasement. V-E Day also emphasised the decline in the nation's fortune from that apogee in June 1944 when Great Britain had a major role in the D-Day landings. Two crippling wars in the first half of the century had almost broken the nation's economy, an economy now expected to fund a welfare state. These were days of butter not guns, and the country's military power would continue its decline over the next 50 years, in the first 35 of which politicians consistently bowed to the political expediency of feeding social programmes on demand.

This book is a record for posterity of the Celebration of Victory at the end of the Second World War in Europe. In order to understand why there was such cause to celebrate war's end, there are four areas to examine in order to help that understanding and set the celebration in its proper context. The first is how the war began in the first place, and the second a very general tracing of the progress of the war in Europe and at home. This all leads to the pinnacle, the manner in which and the reason why the victory was celebrated. Yet, due to the social and political forces set in train during the course of the war, it is not possible to leave the book on the happy note of celebration. A postscript draws together the political and social ramifications of the war.

CAUSES, PREPARATION AND THE BEGINNING OF WAR

In years to come, historians may well see this century's two world wars as a single conflict, where the war-fighting was separated by a political and economic phase. War-fighting is, after all, the extreme form of political manoeuvre; economics can be an equally potent means of coercion just as it is so often the *raison d'être* for armed conflict. Although the First and Second World Wars were different in nature, the causes of the Second were established in the First. The First World War has greater association with the political and military situation today than has the Second. In that respect, the wheel has turned full circle. The First World War was a war of borders and nationalism while the Second was a war of ideology: communism and fascism. It was Germany who was responsible for starting the First World War, just as Germany was responsible for starting the Second. However, it was the treatment of Germany at the Versailles Peace Conference which is so often cited as the principal cause of the Second World War and why, after the cessation of hostilities in 1918, there was still unfinished business in Europe.

Before we approach the heart of the matter, there is one important point to be made in relation to the examination of a national celebration of ultimate victory within the framework of a world war. A nation concentrates its observations and reporting upon what 'our boys' are doing. This can very often give a misleading and distorted view of what actually happened in a given battle or campaign. For example, the British account of the Dardanelles significantly understates the value of the French contribution. By the same token, if you should study village or town war memorials, the list of the dead in the First World War more often than not exceeds that of the Second. That reflects reality – as far as the British are concerned, our military casualties in the First World War were three times that of the Second World War: 2,365,035 to 755,439. Thus there is a general impression within the country that the First World War was significantly more severe in terms of loss of life and property than the Second. That is not so, and it is not so by a wide margin. Approximately 15 million military and 34 million civilians died in the Second World War, perhaps six times more than in the First. The Russians lost 11 million in a war where their contribution has been hugely underestimated. For example, 93 per cent of the casualties suffered by the German military during 1941–1943 were at the hands of the Red Army. The destruction of property in the war was not localised but global. Thus there was much wider interest and justification for the celebration of total victory after a war that, for the original antagonists, had lasted six years. During those six years, there had been working in tandem great social and political undercurrents which had positive influences on the lives of countless millions in western societies and former colonies. They therefore had good cause to celebrate a victory which now enabled change to come about.

The infusion of American manpower into the Western Front in 1918 to break the deadlock also had the effect of increasing the influence of the Democrat President Woodrow Wilson within Europe. France, who had suffered more than any other European nation as a result of Germany's aggression – 1.25 million dead and 700,000 disabled – sought after the war to bring into being an international army and an international General Staff, so that states could be encouraged to set aside their inherent sovereign right to go to war. Wilson blocked any further progress of that initiative because he did not want to see the resurgence of the alliances which had been so instrumental in bringing about the First World War. As an alternative, he introduced his famous and radical Fourteen Points as a blueprint for the future. It was upon the basis of the Fourteen Points that the League of Nations was founded and Germany entered the Paris Peace Conference. However, in blocking the French collective security initiative and not putting in place an alternative, Wilson had been instrumental in creating an international organisation which had no teeth. By now he was gaining a reputation as an ideas man short on detail.

What Germany achieved at Versailles was not what she was led to believe by Woodrow Wilson. His problem was that his idealism had not been tempered by an adequate measure of realism. When war ended and great international politicians and diplomats foregathered, Wilson, who typed out his own directives on an upright machine, was found to be inadequate in the corridors of international summits; so much so that he became marginalised. The fact that Great Britain and France had less need of the USA after the war meant that a European-led solution emerged for the clipping of Germany's wings. The motives were, however, different. France's aims were continentalist in nature while Britain's were global, and this became a source of tension between the two states. France wanted a punitive peace while Britain was more conciliatory, having as her principal aim the rehabilitation of Germany. No sooner was the ink dry on the peace treaty in Versailles than Clemenceau said to Lloyd George, 'within an hour of the Armistice you have become the enemy of France'. Lloyd George looked at him and said evenly, 'is that not always so?'.

For the allies who set out in 1914 on a short, victorious war, the course of the war proved to be an unpleasant shock. Neither Great Britain nor France imagined Germany to be as strong as they found her. Neither country had read correctly the portents of the Russo-Japanese War of 1904–1905 as an indicator of the ferocious nature of modern warfare. It was the reaction to this discovery that influenced French and British approaches to the German problem in the interwar years. Needless to say, they took different courses of action. The end of the First World War also saw the development of those ideologies which would trigger the Second. A new foundation had been laid on which Russia underwent a bloody revolution to embrace Communism. Britain's and France's claims to be great powers had been severely undermined. Austria-Hungary had become history and Turkey, scion of the Ottoman Empire, had become virtually powerless.

The principal decision-makers responsible for the Treaty of Versailles were Great Britain, France and the USA. Once the incidentals of the peace had been stripped away, the core business of the Paris Peace Conference was to provide for future French security, although Great Britain and the USA were cautious not to allow France to become over-inflated. The same was true at the end of the Second World War. The problem of France living alongside a bitter and defeated Germany lay in the excess of resources in Germany's favour. Germany's population was 60 million to France's 40 million, and Germany's economy was four times stronger than France's. The peace strategy, therefore, revolved around measures to emasculate Germany in order to achieve France's peace of mind.

France's concept of strategic and economic equalisation required the detachment of the Rhineland from Germany so as to provide France with a natural line of defence. Her proposal to address the economic imbalance involved the return of Alsace Lorraine and the gaining of the Saarland. The USA's recognition of the dangers of squeezing a potentially revolutionary Germany too hard was reflected in her not demanding reparations. But she had profited from the war while Great Britain and France had suffered great economic hardship and were in need of, and demanded, reparations from Germany. Consequently, a Reparations Committee was established, to report by 1921 what Germany's assessed liability should be. We should re-emphasise here that the USA was the only real winner to emerge from the war in Europe, a war which had been drawn rather than won. Germany's industry and infrastructure had not been damaged. That this fact was uppermost in some people's minds was evident a month after V-E Day in a message from Field Marshal Montgomery to the inhabitants of the British Zone of Germany. The subject was what, on the face of it, was the schoolmasterish sanction of non-fraternisation:

In the last war of 1914, which your rulers began, your army was defeated; your generals surrendered; and in the Peace Treaty of Versailles your rulers admitted that the guilt of beginning the war was Germany's. But the war never came to your country; your cities were not damaged, like the cities of France and Belgium, and your armies marched home in good order. Then your rulers began to spread the story that Germany was neither guilty nor defeated and because the war had not come to your country, many of you believed it, and you cheered when your rulers began another war.

Again, after years of waste and slaughter and misery, your armies have been defeated. This time the allies were determined that you should learn your lesson – not only that you have been defeated, which you must know by now, but that you, your nation, were again guilty of beginning the war. For if that is not made clear to you and your children, you may again allow yourselves to be deceived by your rulers, and led into another war. You are to read this to your children, if they are old enough, and see that they understand.

In 1918 neither Britain nor the USA could contemplate allowing France the Rhineland but instead, as a compensatory measure, they guaranteed France's security, agreed to the demilitarization of the Rhineland, allowing for the occupation of the territory for 15 years. France did gain the Saar coalmines for a period of 15 years, after which, under a League of Nations mandate, there was to be a plebiscite. By far the most important element in this package was the guarantee of France's security by virtue of its deterrent value and potential for the prevention of future war. The manner in which it evaporated was indicative of Wilson's weakness both at home and abroad. The Republican Senate opposed Wilson and, as a consequence, the USA did not join the League of Nations, nor did they ratify the Treaty of Versailles. The security guarantee to France had been linked to the USA's joining of the League of Nations and, since this did not happen, the guarantee never came into being. Great Britain's underwriting of French security was in association with America's. The collapse of the American guarantee therefore removed any British obligation towards France's security.

The peace treaty included measures to deprive Germany of the capacity to wage war. She was permitted a territorial force of 100,000 men but no aircraft, no submarines, no warships above 10,000 tons and no General Staff. These measures, the territorial measures and reparations which, once applied, caused her currency to collapse with consequent massive inflation and unemployment, all collectively contributed to a sense of national humiliation and festering discontent. Domestic issues came to the fore at the war's end as much in Germany as in an isolationist USA and in a Britain trying to make ends meet in the new social environment within a country 'fit for heroes'. By now there were new economic rivals nibbling at Britain's markets but, rather than take them on and develop new, competing technologies, she persevered with old, low technology coal and iron based industries and service industries such as banking and insurance, and plunged even deeper into the depths of the planet to seek out basic markets. The issue of German power had still not been properly addressed.

The 1925 Locarno Treaty provided France with elements of the security guarantee she had sought. Great Britain guaranteed the existing borders of France, Belgium and Germany. Yet Germany remained isolated as a pariah, outside the international community. This was a situation France was keen to perpetuate while Britain's aim in the early 1930s was to assimilate Germany into the world order to allow her to find her own level as a world power. It was the German military who were the foremost objectors to the subjugation of Germany. For them, Hitler's coming to power in 1933 proved serendipitous. They could live with the fact that this Chaplinesque little man had been a corporal in the First World War. Not only did they recognise his power of oratory, but he also offered them what they wanted. He set aside the Versailles restrictions placed upon Germany's military machine.

Meanwhile, in Italy another dictator, in the form of Benito Mussolini, had come to power. He, more than Hitler, convinced himself that he was more powerful than he actually was. Britain's wooing of Italy as a potential ally had nothing to do with a perception of Italy's power but rather with Italy's strategic position in the Mediterranean. Italy's leadership was more impressed by quantity than quality. The army was bigger than they could afford and was poorly led, equipped and trained. Yet they had the Fascist habit of underestimating those they did not respect. With the notable exception of the former Soviet Union, there is a tendency of autocracies to exaggerate their power while democracies behave as though they are weaker than they actually are. Autocrats come to power over the heads of democrats whose apparent weakness can be drawn from the democratic principles enshrined in the freedom of speech. Hitler, for example, was wrong-footed by giving undue credence to the Oxford Union's affirmation that they would not fight for King and Country. The Soviets knew exactly where they stood and, because they had become a closed society, outsiders tended to underestimate their real power. By the mid 1930s the USSR had a fleet of 7,000 tanks and a remarkably effective tank in the T-35. The Germans had their

Germany's architect of 'Blitzkrieg' warfare, General Heinz Guderian.

armour strategist General Heinz Guderian, but the Russians had their Marshal Tukhachevski, that is until 1937 when Stalin had him shot.

France began the 1930s as though she was going to be progressive in her military outlook. Manoeuvres were held with tanks and 10 divisions were motorised. There was still, however, a large body of military opinion in France which shunned the offensive and put its faith behind walls of concrete. The pre-eminent position of the French Army meant that the French Air Force was starved of resources. It had the wrong type and wrong mix of aircraft to take on the Luftwaffe. It is true that France had more tanks than Germany but, given their poor tactical handling, German air superiority and the element of surprise, it all came to nought. The fact that France was unable to intervene when Germany reoccupied the Rhineland in 1936, or come to the aid of her allies during the Czech crisis of 1938, confirmed in the minds of the defence-orientated the wisdom of their strategy. It is true that the Maginot Line on France's eastern border was not breached but, with gaps in Belgium and in the Ardennes, it did not have to be. Britain was becoming increasingly concerned as to her principal ally's competence and capabilities, but she herself was no paragon of military virtue.

At the time the concept of *Blitzkrieg* was being developed in Germany, the British cavalry clung to the horse with grim determination. They, like the Senior Service, were captives of tradition, quite unlike the more egalitarian Royal Air Force, who had barely had time to establish habits, let alone traditions. The British regimental tradition did, admittedly, have strengths but, overall, its insularity and pursuit of parochial interests meant that it, like the Royal Navy, would begin the war in 1939 almost as though nothing had changed since 1918. Marshal of the Royal Air Force Lord Tedder wrote in his memoirs:

Opposite: German troops reoccupying the Rhineland, 1936.

It is our custom and our history to find ourselves involved in war for which we are inadequately equipped and suffering from that mental inertia which lays us open to the charge of habitually thinking in terms of the last war but one. The war which broke out in 1939 found us running true to form.

Technology, however, was bringing about some change, and that was evident from the re-ordering of priorities.

The emerging technology of the 1930s served to enhance the position and importance of air power. This transition was particularly significant for the island nation of Great Britain because it rendered her sea barrier less significant. The absence of land borders with foreign states had been the rationale for being economic with the army and almost entirely reliant upon the Royal Navy to safeguard the islands' security and interests. In 1934, a new strategic analysis was presented by the Defence Re-armament Committee, which recommended that the Defence Budget be equally divided among the three Services. Neville Chamberlain was unconvinced. Stanley Baldwin had said, without the benefit of any evidence, 'the bomber will always get through'. Nevertheless, that is what was believed and hence the assumed political obligation of Neville Chamberlain to adjust the Service priorities. Priority was switched from the already strong navy to the air force.

The RAF's preparedness to attack civilians as legitimate war targets was founded on a broadly held 1920s philosophy. Coincidentally, it presented a useful rationale for building up Bomber Command as a means of breaking the morale of the German population. By the same token, the Air Ministry expected the Germans to hit London hard on Day 1, possibly in a pre-emptive strike. Estimates suggested casualties on the first day would reach 50,000. In fact, throughout the war, casualties on the ground totalled only 150,000. The idea that civilian morale was Germany's Achilles' heel might have had validity within a democracy but it was an extremely naïve concept in a dictatorship. The USAAF's priority of attacking economic targets was more sensible than the RAF's but less sensible than making the right resources available to attack the enemy's armed forces. Whether civilian targets were to be attacked deliberately or whether they became collateral casualties of an attack on economic targets, this large scale involvement of civilians, directly or indirectly, in air attacks was a new departure. In the First World War there had been limited bombing and bombardment of cities and towns. By taking the war to them, the civilian population became uniquely involved and hence acutely interested in the cessation of hostilities, to a degree not previously experienced. Because the war had drawn them into its vortex, they too had real cause to celebrate eventual victory in Europe. The Second World War, therefore, was not just a soldiers' war, it was a people's war, the people fighting in their own way on the Home Front.

There were within the Royal Navy a number who disagreed with contemporary assertions that air power had become predominant. One of these was Admiral Sir Tom Phillips. He maintained that on-board naval armaments would be sufficiently adequate to defeat attacking aircraft. His last command was that of Force Z, sent by Churchill in 1942 to bolster defences in South East Asia. Ships within his task force included HMS *Prince of Wales* and HMS *Repulse*. Both were sunk by Japanese bombers and torpedo-bombers on 10 December 1941 off the east coast of Malaya. Churchill related how the loss of these two fine ships had perhaps greater impact upon him than any other single disaster in the war. There was, of course, his direct involvement in their despatch, but it was also aboard the *Prince of Wales*, early in the war, that he had conferred with President Roosevelt.

The army remained the Cinderella Service. In 1939, Britain had an army of 16 divisions, rather similar in size to the Hungarian army. Excluding those in North Africa, France had 86 divisions, Poland over 40, Germany approximately 125 and the USSR 138. Although

HMS Repulse leaving Singapore Harbour, 8 December 1941.

priorities had shifted, Britain still had a strong fleet in being, as can be seen from the comparative chart below:

	Battleships	*Cruisers*	*Destroyers*	*Submarines*
British Empire	12	54	145	54
Germany	5	8	50	57

It is interesting to note that France had 80 submarines and Italy 105. In September 1939, Germany's front line air strength was 3,609 aircraft, Britain had 1,911 and France 1,792. The significant change from September 1938 was the increase in British reserve aircraft from 412 to 2,200 (Germany had 900). The RAF played their hand shrewdly, for they were extremely wary lest they procure aircraft too soon and thereby risk going to war with obsolescent aircraft. The Germans overtook the RAF's lead position in 1937 and this, together with British developments with radar, served notice to review the situation. Consequently, in 1938 Bomber Command lost their priority to Fighter Command. British factories were quickly geared up so that by the Battle of Britain, British factories were producing 470 fighters a month to Germany's 178. The change of emphasis away from the sea to air was important because within the Axis economies, their armies and navies demanded and received the lion's share of the available money. Both Germany and Japan under-produced on the air resources required to support their strategies, and suffered as a consequence. Economics played a key role in equipment procurement and determining military priorities. In London, the Treasury set itself up as the Controller of Defence Policy, applying the brake on re-armament until it considered the economy had recovered sufficiently after the 1930s depression. The balance of payments deficit in 1931 was £104 million, which reduced in 1937 and 1938 to a deficit of £56 million and £55 million respectively. Not the best of bases from which to wage war.

No examination of the causes of the Second World War can neglect the part played by Adolf Hitler. He was a consequence of a French-inspired policy, condoned by Great Britain, to weaken Germany politically, militarily and economically. He was able to attract the support of moderates because of his promise to restore German prestige and dignity, but his own agenda was more precise.

Mein Kampf reveals a dual aim to purify the race and to find room for expansion for Germany – *Lebensraum*. The formulators of British foreign policy could not comprehend how 'decent' Germans could follow an absurd little racist like Hitler. Long after they had accepted that there was no prospect of talking peace with him, they still attempted to reach a peace dialogue with the German people over his head. The opposition's price for the removal of Hitler, however, was virtually the same territorial additions as those expected by Hitler.

The 'Anschluss' (or 'union') of Germany and Austria. Hitler enters Vienna, March 1938.

Great Britain had three potential enemies: Germany, Japan and Italy. The realisation that the Royal Navy might have to fight in the Atlantic, the Pacific and the Mediterranean rekindled political activity to draw Italy away from the Axis. Once again, the priorities for apportioning limited defence monies changed, the navy now taking precedence over the army. It should be remembered that the unhappy experience of the British Expeditionary Force in France in 1914 had not been forgotten and, politically, could not be contemplated. To cross the Mediterranean off the Royal Navy's list of commitments became a prime foreign policy goal. It was no secret that Italy was as fearful of a German hegemony of Europe as was France. In 1938 Hitler, who was an Austrian by birth, ordered his armies into Austria. The *Anschluss* or union with Austria went ahead without opposition. From a territorial point of view, Germany and Italy now shared a common border. Hence the renewed efforts to reach an accommodation with Mussolini. The only effect of these last minute efforts to win over Italy was the resignation of Anthony Eden.

Encouraged by her success in Austria, Germany looked for her next move in her strategy of gaining *Lebensraum*. The Sudetenland, the border area of Czechoslovakia, had a large German population that claimed it was being victimised by both the Czechs and the

29–30 September 1938. The Munich Agreement, Fascists on the right and Britain and France on the left, was a 'no contest'.

Left to right: British Prime Minister Neville Chamberlain, the French Prime Minister Edouard Daladier, Adolf Hitler, Benito Mussolini and the Italian Foreign Minister Count Ciano.

Neville Chamberlain at Heston Airport on 30 September 1938, a few hours after his meeting with Hitler in Munich. Chamberlain reads from a document signed by Hitler and himself, in which the two leaders had expressed their determination 'to remove possible sources of difference and thus to contribute to assure the peace of Europe.'

Slovaks. The real value of incorporating the Sudetenland into the Third Reich lay in the resources that would be accrued. The Germans used their propaganda machine skilfully to fan the flames of discontent until an armed confrontation occurred on the border. This action prompted the famous, or infamous, journey of Neville Chamberlain to Munich. Hitler was blunt. He told Britain and France that, if he was allowed the Sudetenland, he would make no further territorial claims in Europe. If there was opposition to his claim, he would declare war. Despite having defence obligations with Czechoslovakia, Chamberlain agreed, rationalising his appeasement of Hitler on the grounds that Czechoslovakia was 'a distant country about which we know little'. Chamberlain was in an invidious position. In his heart of hearts he could not justify the start of a world war to prevent Germans who were so desirous, from joining their own kith and kin. Britain was in no position to aid the Czechs and, even if she had made such a gesture, the possibility was that both Germany and Italy would react by declaring war.

In January 1939, Chamberlain went to Rome to try to persuade Mussolini to break with Hitler. By now, the Foreign Office had come to the conclusion that it could not do otherwise than accept that Germany would have a free hand in Eastern Europe. But it was a policy which would not survive Hitler's reneging on the Munich agreement when in March he seized Prague and the remainder of

We, the German Führer and Chancellor and the British Prime Minister, have had a further meeting today and are agreed in recognising that the question of Anglo-German relations is of the first importance for the two countries and for Europe.

We regard the agreement signed last night and the Anglo-German Naval Agreement as symbolic of the desire of our two peoples never to go to war with one another again.

We are resolved that the method of consultation shall be the method adopted to deal with any other questions that may concern our two countries, and we are determined to continue our efforts to remove possible sources of difference and thus to contribute to assure the peace of Europe.

Adolf Hitler

Neville Chamberlain

September 30. 1938

The famous 'scrap of paper' – the Munich Agreement.

Czechoslovakia. That action put the cat among the pigeons. Military staff talks between London and Paris began, and plans were drawn up to do what a few months previously had been unthinkable – sending six British divisions to the Continent. At home, the Territorial Army was doubled and, on 31 March 1939, Great Britain gave Poland an unqualified promise of protection. Meanwhile, in May 1939, the Conscription Bill passed through Parliament, though not without Labour and Liberal Party opposition. By establishing this enabling bill, Parliament set in train the formation of a citizens' army which, after celebrating their ultimate, deserved victory, would look forward to what, in their minds, was overdue social and political reform.

On 21 March, Hitler demanded of Poland the return of the German port of Danzig and freedom of passage to it and to East Prussia through the so-called 'Polish Corridor'. Poland dismissed the German request. Hitler did not treat the British guarantee to Poland lightly but he realised that, without Russia's acquiescence, it was worthless. Britain, however, had been extremely diffident in her dealings with Russia, even spurning an earlier offer to enter into a non-Fascist alliance. Therefore the way was open for Germany to

The Non-Aggression Pact with Soviet Russia during the Polish Crisis of August-September 1939. Molotov signs the Ten Year Non-Aggression Pact with Germany, 23 August 1939.

do a deal with Russia in order to negate the British guarantee of Polish security. On the face of it, a deal between the leading Communist and Fascist states seemed improbable. But, when Hitler's Foreign Minister, Joachim von Ribbentrop, went to Moscow and dangled in front of Stalin the prospect of regaining the territory lost to Poland in the First World War, pragmatism came to bear and ideological differences were set aside. On 23 August 1939, the Soviet Union signed the Molotov-Ribbentrop Non-Aggression Pact with Nazi Germany. This was the last piece to complete the German power jigsaw and, as a result, the balance of power in Europe was immediately transformed. Hitler was now free to invade Poland with impunity, which he duly did nine days later, on 1 September 1939. As a consequence, war with Great Britain and France was inevitable.

The preamble to Hitler's Directive No.1 for the Conduct of the War ran as follows:

> 1. Since the situation on Germany's Eastern frontier has become intolerable and all political possibilities of peaceful set-tlement have been exhausted, I have decided upon a solution by force.
> 2. The attack on Poland will be undertaken in accordance with the preparations made for 'Case White', with such variations as may be necessitated by the build-up of the Army which is now virtually complete.
> The allocation of tanks and the purpose of the operation remain unchanged.
> Date of attack 1st September 1939.
> This time also applies to operations at Gdynia, in the Bay of Danzig, and at the Dirschau Bridge.

Opposite: Hitler's Directive No.1 for the Conduct of the War. Source: Private

Britain and France demanded the immediate withdrawal of German forces from Poland. Berlin did not acknowledge their demand. London and Paris then debated how best they could aid Poland, but did not come to a workable solution. So they sent an ultimatum. Again, it was ignored and, at 11.00 am on Sunday 3 September 1939, Chamberlain broadcast to the people to tell them that, once again, they were at war with Germany. Thus began the bloodiest and most

Der Oberste Befehlshaber der Wehrmacht   Berlin, den 31.8 39.

OKW/WFA Nr. 170 /39 g.K.Chefs. L I

8 Ausfertigungen
2. Ausfertigung.

Weisung Nr. 1

für die Kriegführung.

1.) Nachdem alle politischen Möglichkeiten erschöpft sind, um
auf friedlichem Wege eine für Deutschland unerträgliche La-
ge an seiner Ostgrenze zu beseitigen, habe ich mich zur
gewaltsamen Lösung entschlossen.

2.) Der Angriff gegen Polen ist nach den für Fall Weiss getrof-
fenen Vorbereitungen zu führen mit den Abänderungen, die
sich beim Heer durch den inzwischen fast vollendeten Auf-
marsch ergeben.

Aufgabenverteilung und Operationsziel bleiben unver-
ändert.

Angriffstag: 1.9.39.

Angriffszeit ....

Diese Zeit gilt auch für die Unternehmungen Gdingen -
Danziger Bucht und Brücke Dirschau.

3.) Im Westen kommt es darauf an, die Verantwortung für die Er-
öffnung von Feindseligkeiten eindeutig England und Frank-
reich zu überlassen. Geringfügigen Grenzverletzungen ist
zunächst rein örtlich entgegen zu treten.

Die von uns Holland, Belgien, Luxemburg und der
Schweiz zugesicherte Neutralität ist peinlich zu achten.

- 2 -

In Great Britain the news of the Declaration of War on Sunday, 3 September 1939, was met with universal gloom and despondency.

widespread war the world had known. Britain had entered the First World War with a sense of enthusiasm, yet she entered the Second with an air of deep foreboding, even despondency. The silver lining to the gathering storm clouds was the end to uncertainty and to living in perpetual crisis. She was embarked upon a war on moral, not territorial or economic, grounds, and a war which her leadership was by no means certain could be won. They did not share the man in the street's residual illusion of national power, but on one thing they were unanimous – they would not be dictated to by Herr Hitler. Equally, there were no jingoistic outbursts in Berlin. The people were in a state of shock; they refused to buy newspapers; they did not want to know. They assumed Hitler would work the oracle of brinkmanship and pull off another bloodless miracle. The war Hitler set in train was not the war he anticipated, nor did it occur when he wanted it. In 1938, the allies believed he might be diverted from war. In 1939, they were certain he could not be. In 1938 there had been economic, political, financial and military reasons why Britain was unable to go to war. In 1939, she was obliged to.

The five divisions of the British Expeditionary Force deployed to France where it waited for the thumping it would receive in May

1940. Political initiatives by the British to try to find a way out of war continued during the lull before the storm, September 1939-May 1940. This was, to use an American term, the period of the 'phoney war', but the impression that nothing much happened during these eight months is erroneous. Aircraft production was notched up a number of gears, cryptology improved, the Territorial Army doubled in strength, a Home Guard was formed, the population was prepared and practised for war, while city children were farmed out to homes in the countryside. Of the three Services, it was the Royal Navy that was most heavily engaged over this period including the muddled joint operation in Norway during April and early May 1940. The period of the Phoney War should not be underestimated in its importance to Great Britain.

Here, after the First World War, we have the classic case of the victor demobilising, shifting resources into social and welfare programmes, as well as addressing the real problems of servicing the national debt. The losers, meanwhile, return to the drawing boards in order to ensure they do not lose again. The fact that Germany became a dictatorship was extremely beneficial in terms of military possibilities. Dictators can legitimately go through the pretence of an argument for either guns or butter before coming down on their intended choice. That does not work in democracies, where the inevitable post-war demands are entirely butter-orientated. Demands for peace dividends are as old as war itself. There is, in addition, the advantage the aggressor derives in terms of war-readiness. The 'pocket' battleships, supposedly built to Washington Treaty displacements, were almost fully worked-up, and would have been fully ready had not the speed with which Germany defeated France left her unprepared for the follow-on phase. We can reasonably say that without the Phoney War there would have been no British victory to celebrate. Britain would not have been able to cling on if she had entered the Second World War from a standing start. The Phoney War period enabled her some essential movement out of the blocks.

The state of the south coast anti-aircraft defences, centred on the vital, strategic port of Portsmouth, would have defied the description of the *Dad's Army* scriptwriting team. The Territorial gunners had been mobilised encouragingly early – on Monday 25 September

1938 – only to be stood down, before being mobilised again in 1939. Training proved to be basic and repetitious. The drone of a Tiger Moth biplane told promenaders on the Southsea front that the local gunners were hard at their daily training. The aeroplane, on hire from Portsmouth airport, flew low and straight at 80 miles an hour as a target for the gun crews and predictors. The Luftwaffe's Heinkel bomber, He IIIH-3, flew at 258 miles an hour, but the speed differential was not the only problem. The gunners were not trained in aircraft identification. Their army-issue silhouettes of British aircraft, all single-engined biplanes, were at least 10 years old and therefore worthless. Typical British pragmatism came into play when it was discovered that John Player had issued a series of cigarette cards of aircraft in RAF service. That solved the problem in part, for although the older aircraft's lines were distinct, those of the modern aircraft were drawn in such a manner as to conceal their distinctive features. A member of the unit wrote:

> Most of us had collected a set of these cards and put them to good use. A casual observer, seeing us studying our 'fag cards', would have suffered a rapid and total loss of morale. Not one of us had the smallest idea of the shape and appearance of a single German machine. Dear, wonderful, sloppy old Britain.

The Royal Navy provides a better illustration of British unpreparedness. The best known of the early war, naval disasters were those concerning HMS *Courageous* and HMS *Royal Oak*. The early loss of HMS *Courageous* underlines just how far this, the world's premier navy, had to go to prepare for war and the long haul to ultimate victory. This unfortunate ship was an aircraft carrier, sunk in the western approaches on 17 September 1939. The story is told through the correspondence and writing of a Canadian pilot, Lieutenant Hank Rotherham, and a sailor, Lieutenant George Best.

HMS *Courageous* and HMS *Ark Royal* were both fleet carriers supported by a number of destroyers. The theory was that the carriers would act as bait for submarines. The anti-submariners were no different from the other interest groups within the Royal Navy in making inflated claims as to their own ability. They were supremely confident that sonar-equipped destroyers, supported by air cover, would have no difficulty in detecting and sinking submarines. They grossly overestimated their capacity to find U-boats. This particular vignette begins on 14 September 1939 with HMS *Ark Royal* and her pack of shepherding destroyers operating west of the Hebrides.

In the same waters was the U-39, equipped with torpedoes armed with magnetic pistols. These particular torpedoes proved to be particularly unreliable in the higher latitudes, exploding prematurely, as would be the case again off Norway. The U-39's attack on the *Ark Royal* failed for that reason. The ship's counter measures worked reasonably well, her Blackburn Skua dive bombers sinking the U-39, but not before one had brought itself down with its own anti-submarine bomb. The *Ark Royal* was enormously lucky to escape the attack of the U-39, for she played a vital role in the first two years of the war at sea. She was lucky, the *Courageous* unlucky.

Hank Rotherham joined a squadron of Swordfish torpedo attack aircraft forming at Gosport Air Station. Their time was taken up not with training but with getting the biplanes ready to fly. Once out of storage they had to be completely overhauled, engines run up and tuned, radios installed and compasses checked – something that was really vital when reconnoitring over the sea, far from land and up to

Aerial view of HMS Courageous with an escort plane guard destroyer on her port quarter.

HMS Courageous taking on board the last of the wayward Swordfish after her fateful detour. The smoke suggests that she may already have been torpedoed.

100 miles away from the carrier, in visibility that could be down to a few miles. Preparing the squadron took a long time. There were insufficient batteries for the radios, so the pilots had to go into Portsmouth to buy them from the shops. Meanwhile, *Courageous* was coming out of the dockyard and was immediately commissioned. *Courageous* and *Glorious* (sunk by *Scharnhorst* and *Gneisenau*, 8 June 1940) represented Admiral Fisher's concept of light cruisers. They were therefore First World War battle cruisers, converted into carriers by the addition of a flight deck. The point is, they were not sturdy ships.

In a couple of weeks, the Swordfish squadron assigned to *Courageous* was ready, with the requisite pilots and most of the observers. They flew to Devonport to join their ship. They had time only to begin reconnaissance flights before war was declared. *Courageous* was not trained up for war as a ship, and her torpedo squadron was untrained in the art of dropping torpedoes. They had no option but to compromise and adopt the high pattern bombing method of attack. All too soon, *Courageous* put to sea. Convoys had not been introduced, and there were many slow merchantmen moving independently; ideal targets for U-boats. The Admiralty required *Courageous* to fly anti-submarine patrols to try to keep the German

HMS Courageous sinking. The list accounts for the high number of officers and crew lost.

submarines down. The carrier had four destroyers as an anti-submarine screen. On 17 September, one of the Swordfish sighted a submarine. The Captain (D) (the overall commander of destroyers in the Carrier Group) persuaded *Courageous*'s captain, Captain W T Mackaig-Jones, that two destoyers were sufficient to protect *Courageous*. He steamed off into the Atlantic with the other two destroyers. 'I am afraid', wrote Hank Rotherham, 'that the call of fame must have overpersuaded him to ease up on his main objective – the safety of *Courageous*.'

As was the case with the U-39 and *Ark Royal*, it was not a coincidence that the U-29 was in the same waters as *Courageous*. The Germans were reading the Admiralty's signals traffic. *Courageous* steamed past the U-29, just outside the range of her torpedoes. However, two of *Courageous*'s Swordfish were overdue and the captain altered course 100 degrees until they were located. The change of course took *Courageous* towards the German submarine. In exercising the turn, the inadequate destroyer screen fell behind, rather than being ahead to locate submarines. Captain Mackaig-Jones steadied up again into the wind to take aboard the two Swordfish. The German commander, watching through his periscope, could not believe his good fortune. *Courageous* was a sitting duck. He ordered the torpedoes *'los!'*. Hank Rotherham commented sagely: 'These moments of complete insecurity are fleeting but they exist and can be disastrous, as we found'.

Over a year later, on 7 November 1940, Hank Rotherham wrote an account of the sinking of *Courageous* in a letter to his brother-in-law:

I was in the chart house, on the Bridge, at the time of the explosion, it really was a very big shaking and all the lights went out. Within a few minutes the ship had a very big list on and we had to hold on to prevent ourselves slipping down the decks. There was no sign of any panic, and indeed there was considerable relish at the prospect of a weekend leave as a result. The list was so big that it was very difficult to get rafts and boats out, particularly as there was no electric power. I made my way down the starboard side, it was about as easy to stand on the side of the ship as on the deck, and took up a position on the starboard bilges with many others. While I was there a young seaman came down with a large grin all over his face and told me with joy that he had seen our submarine sunk. By this time the ship was right down by the bows and with a heavy list of about 35° to port. Just before she went, one of the boats on the port side came afloat while still on its davits and two men swam back and unhooked her. She was holed by the ship as she went, but saved a number of men, who bailed to keep her afloat. Rather a stout effort, as the ship was towering over them, and coming lower and lower.

Eventually, 19 minutes after we were struck, the ship started to go quite quickly and quite definitely. We all took off from the side, and I did one of my fastest 50 yards away from the ship. I then turned and watched. The bows went right down and she finally plunged almost vertically with a rushing noise. It was a most impressive sight to see the stern right up in the air, men still dropping off, and her four screws stopped, coming down fast. I should not have cared to be under them, one or two were. There were two men standing on the sternpost, waving.

Then rafts and wood started popping up, and one felt glad to be away from her as they came up darned fast, however once up they were most acceptable. We had several friends, one destroyer picking up men, one keeping *cave* for other submarines, and a little Ellerman Line, the *Dido*, who stopped and helped. It was a slow job, as men were strewn about the ocean, and those of us who were late indulged in a little song to keep ourselves cheerful. The water was quite warm (61°) but it began to get a bit cold after half an hour or so swimming about and holding on to bits of wood. Eventually I clambered on board the *Dido* and got some dry clothes in the form of the Captain's trousers (height 5'2") and the Chief Officer's coat. The *Dido*'s men stripped themselves to the skin, one of the crew took off his trousers to give to one of our officers. They really were magnificent, as they themselves did not know that the submarine had been sunk. [In fact the Captain (D's) claim had been wishful thinking. U-29 escaped.]

One of our men in *Dido* had had a foot nearly torn off as the ship went down and there was no anaesthetic on board. Luckily our young Doc was with us, and so he was given a teaspoon of opium and then three of us held him down while Doc sewed the foot on again. I say, held him down, but it was not necessary, he had a bandage to chew and me to hold on to and we three just steadied him, not a squeak or struggle.

Why was it, therefore, that one torpedo (as was claimed by a number of survivors) sank an aircraft carrier with the loss of 518 lives including the captain? It was redolent of a navy not having sorted itself out, of suspect damage control, but, more particularly, due to the nature of the crew. '*Courageous*', explained Hank Rotherham,

was largely manned by pensioners and reservists – men who had done their time and retired to live on their retired pay and spend much of their days in the pub. During my career in the war, I far preferred an ambitious amateur to a retired pro . . . I am sure that this lack of energy was, in part at least, the reason why so many did not get out of the ship, though we must remember the terrible list which developed so quickly and must have made it hell down below with everything falling about and many ladders vertical.

Another reason for the high loss of life was that there were few life jackets aboard. Many of those that were had been chewed to pieces by rats. Hank, who was an accomplished water polo man, handed his over to a petty officer. The problem was, the pensioners were from a time when the lower decks were not encouraged to swim. This presented the *Courageous*'s Dartmouth-trained officers with an enormous quandary. George Best, in a letter to his sister Peg dated 23 September 1939, stated that he left *Courageous* late 'for one reason or another'. This was due to his heroic efforts to get the men to budge.

> It was pathetic seeing them sitting on the 'bilges' just before we foundered, being unable to decide whether to jump and drown, or hold on tight and get it over quickly. It was they who made me late – I was helping to look for wood for them, but it had all gone.

Lieutenant Best decided that he could do no more and leapt into the water. He had only got 20 yards clear of the ship when she foundered, sucking him down with her:

> I thought it was the end, but for some reason I wasn't frightened: I went down, and down, and down. Then my foot came up against part of the ship, and I gave a good shove off. I then saw the water getting lighter and lighter until I finally broke surface: but just not long enough to get a breath, for I then went under again. I was hurled head over heels in a mad career round the ocean – not deep down, but below the surface for far longer than I cared. At last I came up, to find a terrific turbulent sea gradually subsiding into the ordinary, long, heavy Atlantic swell. And did I breathe!

Meanwhile, Hank Rotherham was in the water, swimming strongly away from the ship to avoid being sucked down.

> I was swimming towards a raft when I came across a couple of young men, neither a good swimmer, who were in trouble. I got hold of the nearest, but was then grappled by the other. A lit-

tle roughness got me away from him. Then I said, "I can't take you both", and he let go, making no more attempt to get hold of me. I took the first to the raft and then looked back. He had gone. A brave man who followed the example of Captain Oates.

A quarter of the ship's officers perished, most of them competent swimmers who gave their lives endeavouring to save their men.

The impact of the loss of the *Courageous* on the people at home was enormous. The Captain (D), also Captain of HMS *Inglefield*, spent four days after the loss of *Courageous* hunting submarines and returning to base. None of the relatives of the crew of the *Courageous* he had taken on board knew that they had survived. The Captain had said that he was prepared to signal the names of the officer survivors but not the men, because the list would be too long. The *Courageous*'s officers declined to have their names radioed ahead. This was a nightmare which many wives and mothers underwent throughout the war, the news of the loss of a ship often preceding the list of casualties.

As soon as he got ashore, Hank telephoned his wife. After hanging up, his wife Debbie rushed outside and onto the adjoining golf course, where the family doctor was teeing up. The man was more than a little perplexed to be seized and kissed by this excitable woman. Once he had recovered his composure and heard Mrs Rotherham's good news, he said: 'I am looking forward to such another event without wishing your husband any real harm'. When he got home to a family welcome, Hank still had the Captain of *Dido*'s trousers and First Officer's coat, given to him when he was pulled, cold and dripping, from the sea. When his mother took them into the dry cleaners at Godalming, the man behind the counter remarked on the oil and dirt, to which Mrs Rotherham senior said they had come out of the *Courageous*. The man's reply sums up the attitude and feelings of the people at home. 'Madam, they will be cleaned and there will be no charge. I owe it to the country.'

A month later HMS *Royal Oak*, an old First World War R-class battleship, was at anchor on 14 October 1939 in the protected fleet anchorage of Scapa Flow. The crew was aboard and therefore bulkhead doors were open. The German submarine U-47 under Captain Günther Prien entered the harbour and, in the first few minutes of 15 October, hit the battleship with one torpedo, which caused no damage and, surprisingly, no reaction from those aboard. Thirty minutes later, Prien put three torpedoes into the battleship. She sank in 13 minutes, having capsized, and took 833 of her officers and crew down with her.

By May 1940, the leadership crisis in Britain had come to a head. In the House of Commons, Chamberlain faced the most virulent attacks for his misplaced optimism for peace and for his appeasement of Hitler. Foes and friends alike turned upon him, a political scapegoat. A former friend, Leo Amery, struck a Cassius-blow at his leader, quoting from Cromwell: 'You have sat here too long for any good you have been doing. Depart, I say, and let us have done with you! In the name of God, go!' There followed the unison chants around the House, 'Go! Go! Go!' Chamberlain, humbled and devastated, resigned. On 10 May, the King called for Winston Churchill to lead a national government to prosecute the war. On that same day, Germany invaded Holland, Belgium and Luxembourg. The nation's morale soared, but the by now pathetic Chamberlain had been hard done by. In 1938-39, his policy of appeasement was an entirely realistic policy for a state with neither the resources nor the power to counter the threat posed by Germany. He was no weak, misguided, craven man, but a realist who saw Britain's power in its true light rather than as it was seen by a majority imbued with the illusion of an impressive, national power. The future struggle would be long and hard and would not be won without powerful allies. The final victory and celebration was far in the future.

BEARING THE STRAIN

In one of the most comprehensive defeats of one nation by another, the German *Blitzkrieg* forced France into submission in six weeks. France was obliged to sign the Armistice with Germany in the same railway carriage in Compiègne as Germany had signed the Armistice in 1919. There were other similarities which made the point – the French Army, for example, had a ceiling of 100,000 men placed upon it. This defeat created enormous difficulty for Great Britain, strategically dependent as she was upon France's existence. A number in the British government recognised that Britain and the Empire could not defeat Nazi Germany unaided and seriously questioned whether hostilities should continue. Lord Halifax, Foreign

The railway carriage used for the signing of the Armistice of France at Compiègne in 1940 had been brought to Berlin as a trophy. It was later destroyed in Allied air raids.

Secretary, recommended that Hitler should be sounded out through the conduit of Mussolini as to what might be possible. It was certainly within the realms of possibility that Great Britain might have come to the conclusion that the least bad option would be to join a National Socialist Co-Prosperity Sphere.

Coincidentally, these diplomatic overtures coincided with the death throes of France and the BEF's becoming surrounded in and around the port of Dunkirk. Hitler ordered his Panzers to withhold the *coup de grâce*, in part because they needed to regroup but also, presumably, because of Britain's ongoing peace overtures. Planners thought it might be possible to evacuate 30,000 soldiers over the beaches but, due to Hitler's intervention, the little boats brought back from the beaches of Belgium and France a total of 338,226 Allied soldiers. This tipped the balance of possibilities. Privately, Churchill believed that he still might have to enter into a negotiated settlement with Hitler but, if he could persuade the dictator that Britain could not be defeated, he might achieve a better deal. Publicly,

Dunkirk. Hitler restrained the German armed forces from engaging the remnants of the Allied forces surrounded in the region of Dunkirk.

As a result, 338,226 were hurriedly evacuated to fight another day.

he maintained a pugnacious profile, broadcasting to the nation after the deliverance of the BEF one of the most famous speeches ever delivered in the English language. The American broadcaster Ed Murrow said, 'he mobilised the language and made it fight':

> We shall go on to the end. We shall fight in France, we shall fight on the sea and oceans, we shall fight with growing confidence and growing strength in the air; we shall defend our island whatever the cost may be. We shall fight on the beaches, we shall fight on the landing-grounds, we shall fight in the fields and in the streets, we shall fight in the hills; we shall never surrender.

He went on to say how Britain and the Empire would carry on the struggle and then said, pointedly, 'until in God's good time, the New World, with all its power and might, steps forth to the rescue and liberation of the Old'. Churchill sent the pro-appeasement Lord Halifax off to be ambassador to Washington. Halifax was a competitor, an alternative prime minister. Had Halifax, rather than Churchill, become prime minister, there may well have been little for the nation to celebrate. The United States' ambassador in London, Joseph Kennedy, was no friend of this country. 'England will go down fighting', he once said. 'Unfortunately I am one who does not believe it is going to do the slightest bit of good.' With Halifax and Kennedy in place, there is little wonder that Churchill so often chose to talk directly to President Roosevelt.

Hitler's dilatoriness had handed Britain a fighting chance and, since Churchill had made his situation unequivocal, on 16 July Hitler issued Führer Directive 16, the orders to prepare the seaborne attack on Britain, Operation SEA LION, to begin on 15 September.

> Since England, in spite of her hopeless military situation, shows no signs of being ready to come to an understanding, I have decided to prepare a landing operation against England, and, if necessary, to carry it out. The aim of this operation will be to eliminate the English homeland as a base for the prosecution of war against Germany and, if necessary, to occupy it completely.

The Royal Navy still ruled the waves around Britain's coast, the German navy being unable to challenge her pre-eminent position directly. To have six German divisions at sea was a risky business unless air superiority could be guaranteed, and here lay the nub or the rationale for the Battle of Britain. Hitler ordered Hermann Goering to plan a massive air assault as a preliminary to the invasion by sea. By engaging the Royal Air Force in the air and on the ground, it was intended to cause such attrition of her limited resources as to enable the German barges to cross over to England unhindered. But the Luftwaffe was unprepared. So rapid had been Germany's success in France that the Luftwaffe had not developed her strategic bombing techniques. Radar was much further developed in Britain than in Germany and this enabled the RAF's fighter control at Uxbridge to detect the incoming bombers and give the fighters up to 30 minutes' warning. The switch of priority from bombers to fighters in 1938 was one of the inspirational decisions of the prewar period. Fighters of the Royal Air Force operating from their airfields in southern England, and hence having significant loiter time, had no

Germany prepared barges on the French coast for Operation SEA LION, the invasion of Great Britain. This photo was taken in Boulogne.

difficulty intercepting the slow German bombers operating at the extremity of the range of their fighter support.

At the beginning of the Battle of Britain, the RAF had a mixed bag of aircraft. There were 46 squadrons of Spitfire and Hurricane day-time fighters, and eight squadrons of Defiants and Blenheims. This meant that there were approximately 800 serviceable fighters although the Defiants, Blenheims and, to some degree, the Hurricanes, were no match for the principal German fighter, the Messerschmitt Bf 109E-1. Consequently the tactics invariably sent the Hurricanes against the incoming bombers while the Spitfire took on the direct fuel injection Bf 109E-1s. The situation was described by Flying Officer Jeffrey Quill in Norman Gelb's book *Scramble*:

> When the battle heated up, the job of the Spitfire squadron was to climb up, engage the German fighter escort and let the bombers go by. We'd take off and be vectored out. We'd see a bloody great formation of Dorniers coming in at 12,000 feet. We'd be told to ignore them. Up above were their fighter escorts. Our job was to get up and engage those fighters, get a good old dogfight going, get everything milling around, during which time the bombers would be groaning inexorably along. With any luck, by the time they got anywhere near the target, we'd have forced all their escort fighters out of position and down would come our Hurricanes to get at those bombers. That was the general idea. The Spitfire and the Hurricane complemented each other. They were an ideal couple, provided we could handle the battle that way. The two aircraft together – plus the radar – those were the things that won the Battle of Britain.

The Luftwaffe had available 1,000 Messerschmitt fighters including some of the less successful Bf 110C-4. Where the major imbalance occurred was in the number of available pilots. In 1940, the Luftwaffe had 10,000 trained pilots, many with operational experience in Spain, while Fighter Command had only 1,450 and was training a mere 50 a week. A sergeant pilot remembered what his squadron leader had said: 'You've got to shoot down four enemy planes before you're shot down yourself because that's what the odds are. Otherwise, you're wasting your time'. If Hitler maintained a policy of striking at Fighter Command in the air and on the ground he would, through the process of attrition, win the Battle of Britain.

The main phase of the Battle of Britain began on 11 August when the Luftwaffe attacked fighter bases around the periphery of London, the radar stations at Ventnor and atop the White Cliffs of Dover, as well as shipping in the Thames Estuary. The Ventnor station was badly damaged in the raid and a number of airfields were put out of action for a short period. Ominously, the RAF and Luftwaffe losses were roughly equal. Goering was keen to demonstrate to the Führer the Luftwaffe's supremacy over the RAF, and this crushing display of superiority and strength was scheduled for *Adlertag* or Eagle Day. Bad weather postponed Eagle Day until 13 August but the 1,500 attacks on that day were not as substantial as the 1,786 sorties launched from France, Germany and Norway on 15 August. The German targets were the RAF fighter bases in Kent, Sussex, Hampshire, Hull and Newcastle. In the air battle that day,

A Hurricane I fighter of 601 Squadron being serviced prior to the next operation.

Scramble! Spitfire pilots race to their aircraft to intercept incoming 'bandits'.

the RAF lost 34 fighters and the Luftwaffe 108. The RAF's advantage of fighting 'at home' meant that if an aircraft was damaged, it was only a short hop to one of the many southern airfields or, if baling out was unavoidable, it was invariably done over friendly territory. A high proportion of the Luftwaffe's damaged aircraft ended their return flights in the English Channel.

German Intelligence realised that every attack launched against Fighter Command would weaken it. On 16 August, an attack similar to the previous day's was launched, and again and again. The Luftwaffe's Intelligence estimated the RAF fighter strength to be down to 300, and returning pilots were particularly questioned as to whether gaps in the RAF's fighter strength were now apparent. The answer was negative. The German pilots reported the RAF to be as strong as ever. There were 600 front line fighters on the airfields of England, but there were not 600 fighter pilots. Fortunately, the radar system proved to be a vital force multiplier, guiding the limited fighter assets to where they were most needed. Because German intelligence overestimated the RAF's losses, they no longer considered the radar sites to be prime targets and they were left alone to conduct their battle-winning function. By the end of the third week in August, the Luftwaffe had lost over 450 aircraft.

On 24 August, some disorientated Luftwaffe bombers jettisoned their bombs over London. Incensed, Churchill ordered the retaliatory bombing of Berlin. The Germans, still hopeful of a peace settlement, had forbidden the indiscriminate bombing of London. They were content to concentrate on their principal target, namely Fighter Command. Goering was furious when he heard of the unauthorised bombing of London:

> An immediate report is required identifying those crews who dropped bombs within the perimeter of London. Luftwaffe High Command will itself undertake the punishment of each aircraft captain involved.

The punishment was draconian. 'They will be posted to infantry regiments.' Goering did not hold Bomber Command in high regard. He once boasted: 'If the RAF bomb Berlin you can call me Braun'. Hitler was outraged by the attack on his capital city by an air force supposedly on its last legs. It was at this point that Hitler's indignation got the better of his judgement, for he ordered Goering to switch the Luftwaffe's bombers from the fighter bases in southern England to attack British cities. On 7 September, the attacks began.

The first raid by 1,000 aircraft took London and the ground and air defences by surprise. London and her docks were bombed, and 1,600 civilians were killed or injured. The attack on the people's morale did not succeed. In fact the contrary was true, it merely strengthened their resolve to persevere. Edward Murrow's broadcast on 10 September for CBS Radio News reported:

> We are told today that the Germans believe Londoners, after a while, will rise up and demand a new government, one that will make peace with Germany. It's more probable that they'll rise up and murder a few German pilots who come down by parachute. The life of a parachutist would not be worth much in the East End of London tonight.

That same Cockney spirit was seen across the land as the Luftwaffe bombers spread their net to include the cities on the South Coast, the Midlands and the North. The switching to night air attacks tested the RAF to the extreme because there was no suitable airborne interception radar, and it would take a number of months to overcome that particular difficulty. Hitler's original purpose in attacking Fighter Command directly, and then indirectly by bombing London, had been to clear the way for Operation SEA LION. But here was the Luftwaffe, as late as 15 September, returning from a bombing raid having lost over 60 aircraft (the RAF claimed to have shot down 185). The RAF lost 26 fighters but recovered half the pilots. 15 September marked the effective end of the Battle of Britain. Two days later, Hitler called off Operation SEA LION indefinitely, the invasion barges were dispersed, and the threat disappeared. In the House of Commons on 20 August, Churchill demonstrated that he had lost none of his gift of rhetoric: 'Never in the field of human conflict was so much owed by so many to so few'. Hitler would never know quite how few there had been. Of the original 1,450 fighter pilots, one third died in the battle and a further third were wounded.

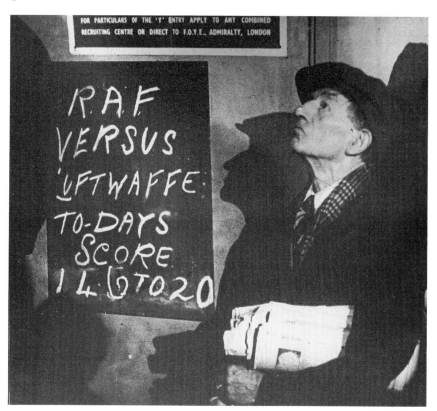

The RAF's claim of kills during the Battle of Britain was exaggerated. It was, however, powerful medicine for the morale of the people.

It was cold comfort for the civilians on the Home Front that Hitler switched the emphasis from Fighter Command to British cities when he did, but in doing so he kept alive the flicker of hope that the people of these islands would emerge victorious.

The loss of 2,000 Luftwaffe aircraft was too high a price to pay to defeat an obstinate race living at the periphery of Hitler's grand design. Defeating Britain was not Hitler's principal aim. It is just that having defeated France, the next obvious step was to remove the threat posed by Britain before turning back to the main objective of the war. Mesmerised as he was, he ignored the lessons of Napoleon's defeat and prepared to follow Germany's destiny by attacking his ideological enemy, Russia. It was not, however, just ideology which caused him to overturn the expedient Molotov-Ribbentrop pact. It was also to do with economics and *Lebensraum*. Operation BARBAROSSA began on 22 June 1941 with three German thrusts into Russian territory. By that action, Hitler had provided Britain with one of her two major allies. The second, the USA, became an ally in December 1941 when Germany declared war on her. A very important decision was then reached with the USA in 1942, that the priority of resource allocation should be the European theatre and, once Germany had been defeated, all the available men and equipment would be concentrated to defeat Japan.

Thus, by the end of 1941, the alliance that would secure eventual victory in Europe and the Far East was in place. Yet it was a relationship which caused the British some severe difficulties, both before and after V-E Day. Churchill commented upon the difficulties of fighting wars with allies, but added that wars were more difficult to fight without them. The British relationship with Russia was one of minimal contact, coolness, and suspicion borne of a fear of subversion. Churchill was much keener to pursue substantive links with the 'New World'. His mother was American and, in 1943, he coined a phrase that 'a special relationship' existed between Great Britain and the USA. However, the Americans nurtured a hidden agenda which had its origins in the economic rivalry existing between the two states as well as the desire that Britain would emerge from the war a weaker power. America felt threatened, not only by the sterling area but also by imperial preference. The cost of confronting Hitler had emptied Britain's coffers and she needed loans in order

The Battle for Stalingrad. In the outskirts of Stalingrad a German light infantry gun unit brings its gun into action.

to continue the war. America came forward with her famous lend-lease programme in order to permit Britain to continue the fight. There was no option but to accept lend-lease. It was the only offer available, yet it was also a poisoned chalice. Lend-lease was not a cash-oriented, private loans programme, but required the $27 billion loan repaid in kind. Already, half of Great Britain's balance of payments deficit was due to the USA. The price for lend-lease was the abandonment of the sterling area, imperial preference, and the making available of British bases. These considerations ensured that Britain's economic foundation at war's end was unable to face both the repayment of deficits accrued during the course of the war as well as lay down a strong social programme for the future. India also demanded payment from Britain for her war-time contribution. At war's end, Britain was the world's largest debtor nation, whereas in 1939 she had been the second largest creditor. Her prospects of climbing out of the economic morass were stymied because the international system did not return to stability but shifted from one form of instability into another.

HMS Brighton, a former US Navy Clemson class destroyer, built in 1919 and a tangible manifestation of lend-lease.

The problem of two theatres of operation – Europe and the Far

Gordon Highlanders of the Eighth Army cross into Tunisia, 17 February 1943.

East – and the understanding, or rather misunderstanding, implicit in 'Europe First', meant that there was no long-term strategy. Even within Europe there were major disagreements among the allies as to strategic priorities. Winston Churchill's capacity to exasperate the French in the Great War, with his attraction to the indirect approach, caused no less difficulty for the Americans in the Second World War. The fact that Britain had been in the war from the beginning, had held the ring on the Western Front, and was the centre for military operations against Europe, had afforded her a position at the high table of operational command which arguably she no longer deserved. Nevertheless, Italy's East African colonies had already been captured in the first half of 1941 and major battles had taken place in Libya with great success, at least until the advent of Rommel and the failure of Wavell's attempt to save Greece from the Germans. Then in October and November 1942, Montgomery defeated Rommel at El Alamein. North Africa was invaded by the Allies and there soon followed the first invasion of the European mainland through Sicily and Italy. All this took place while Hitler invaded the Soviet Union in June 1941 and made deep advances into her territory as far as the outskirts of Leningrad and Moscow and eventually Stalingrad, which would prove to be his Waterloo.

In the Far East, the Japanese declared war in December 1941, bombed Pearl Harbor, drove the British out of Hong Kong, Malaya, Singapore and most of Burma, and the Dutch out of their East Indies. Great naval battles were fought in the Pacific, and India and Australia were threatened.

British soldiers, ships and places played a major part in much of this fighting, except in the Soviet Union, and in January 1943 Britain's position was confirmed by what was, for her, the favourable proceedings of the January 1943 Casablanca Conference. The conference had permitted the British a final Indian summer before the sun set on her empire (which was another American foreign policy goal). The Americans came away having achieved less than they felt they deserved, and some with an attitude problem which lasted for

Tanks and a jeep of 4th Brigade entering the shattered ruins of Cassino, Italy, 18 May 1944.

The January 1943 Casablanca Conference. American President Franklin D. Roosevelt and British Prime Minister Winston Churchill seen with their Service representatives.

the duration of the war. Although the supreme commander was General Dwight D. Eisenhower, emphasising America's position as *primus inter pares,* significant sea, land and air command appointments were held by British officers with Americans under command. What else established the Casablanca Conference as one of rather more than passing importance was Roosevelt's unilateral declaration requiring Germany's unconditional surrender.

Back home, the Battle of Britain had drawn some of the Luftwaffe's sting, but bombing continued and over a wider area. There was, however, another battle being fought and this one, 'The Battle of the Atlantic', was not only equally perilous, but it was also longer lasting. Churchill wrote in his memoirs that: 'The only thing that ever really frightened me during the war was the U-boat peril'. Fortunately, at the beginning of the war, Germany was not organised to start an all-out U-boat campaign. She possessed only 57 submarines, of which 30 were ocean-going types and only six could be on station at any one time. The latter problem was partly symptomatic of operating from the distant Baltic and North Sea ports; a situation which radically changed when France fell, making available the French Atlantic ports to the Germans. Up until that stage the credit/loss ratio was roughly in balance. The Merchant Navy's losses were made up by acquisitions from neutral states and, for every five U-boats the Germans were building each month, they lost three.

Admiral Karl Dönitz's aim was to starve Britain into surrender. Many of the raw materials required to maintain the war effort, not least of which was the building of warships and merchant ships, had to be imported. Great Britain possessed no fuel oil of its own and in 1939 imported half of its food. On the domestic front, immediate economies were imposed to reduce the dependancy upon imports. Petrol and food were rationed, and clothes could only be purchased when supported by clothing coupons. The people were implored to

Rationing was an early measure imposed to reduce the dependency upon imports.

'Dig for Victory'. The smallest pieces of land were taken into cultivation and animals reared for slaughter. Obviously those in the country did rather better than those who remained in the cities.

In 1939, Britain's Merchant Navy was 160,000 strong. Almost 100 per cent British, they manned approximately 3,000 ocean-going vessels and a further 1,000 coastal vessels. Although it was the world's largest merchant fleet, it was not a fleet of over-large proportions in relation to its tasks. The sailors were civilians required to volunteer for war duty. They were extraordinary; the unsung heroes of the war, suffering great loss of life to keep the nation's life blood flowing.

Whereas the pieces in the Battle of the Atlantic were obviously the vulnerable merchantmen, their often inadequate escorts, the occasional proactive air sortie and the U-boats hunting in packs, their guiding fortunes were determined by how good or how bad the Germans and the British were in the fields of code-breaking and cryptology. The Royal Navy employed a code book to control the movements of convoys. That code had been broken very early in the war, yet the Royal Navy persisted in its use, not associating the by now routine interception of its convoys with the compromise of its code book. Dönitz's submarines were meticulous in their use of an encryption device known as Enigma. This machine was used by the Germans to encypher their top secret messages. A word used in association with Enigma was 'Ultra'. This was the intelligence the Allies derived from breaking those cyphers.

The Enigma machine resembled a large typewriter. Its function was to transpose every letter in a message into another letter. Thus the message remained the same length but it went in as German and came out garbled. The original machine was invented and patented in Holland in 1919. The German navy developed an interest in Enigma in 1926, followed by the army in 1929, followed in turn by the Luftwaffe, the police, the SS and the railways. The Polish secret service was reading the German Enigma traffic from 1932 to 1938. After the Münich Conference in September 1938, the Enigma machine was upgraded by the addition of extra rotors and, as a consequence, defied the Polish efforts to read the German traffic. By now, the dark clouds were hanging over Poland and, for what might be seen as a *quid pro quo* for the guarantee of British support, Polish know-how was transferred to the British.

Opposite: Not even the surrounds of the Albert Memorial were sacrosanct when it came to the production of that 'little extra' in the overall concept of 'Dig for Victory'.

Bletchley Park, Buckinghamshire. Source: Private

Ultra was developed to provide land, sea and air intelligence, yet the priority was given to the Battle of the Atlantic. By the end of 1943, the Germans employed 40 different cyphers, all of which required different settings on the Enigma machine. The British code-breakers were established in a country house in Buckinghamshire – Bletchley Park. It was a community of debs and dons which, by the end of the war, numbered 11,000. The people at Bletchley Park worked under enormous pressures and great emotional strain. The historian Peter Calvocoressi explained:

> Even with the exceptional resources available at that location and at that time, it would take the experts several days and in some cases up to a week to find the solution for a particular day's settings to the Enigma machine.

In the first part of 1941, the code-breakers had worked extremely hard to decypher the naval codes, but to no avail. Then, in May 1941 they had the considerably good fortune to receive material detailing the setting of the naval codes taken from a German weather trawler and a cypher machine, with all its supporting material, taken from a captured submarine, the U-110. The impact of this intelligence material was immediate. In the period February-June 1941, 242 ships (1,324,813 tonnes) were sunk. In the period July-November 1941, the figure had fallen to 143 ships (596,069 tonnes). Ultra's contribution as an element in the ultimate victory cannot be quantified. It can only be imagined as considerable and instrumental in reducing the length of the war in Europe.

An Enigma machine —
the four-wheel version in use
with the German Navy from
March 1943.
Source: Private

```
TO I D 8 G                                    ZTP/1054
FROM GERMAN NAVAL SECTION G C AND C S


110/4595 KC/S                          TOI 0025/27/5/41
                      TOO 0153
TO  FLEET W 70
ENEMY REPORT:
TO C IN C AFLOAT:
I THANK YOU IN THE NAME OF THE ENTIRE GERMAN PEOPLE.  ADOLF
HITLER
TO THE CREW OF THE BATTLESHIP BISMARCK:
ALL GERMANY IS WITH YOU.  ALL THAT CAN STILL BE DONE, WILL BE
DONE.  YOUR DEVOTION TO DUTY WILL FORTIFY OUR PEOPLE IN THEIR
STRUGGLE FOR EXISTENCE.  ADOLF HITLER.

TOO 2229/29/5/41+++AGT+++
```

A Bletchley Park translation of a German message from Hitler to Admiral Lütjens and Bismarck's doomed crew. Ten hours later, the Bismarck went down.

Crown Copyright. Reproduced with the permission of the Controller of Her Majesty's Stationery Office.

Margaret 'Hetty' Bowers was one of the analysts working on anti-submarine operations at Bletchley Park.

We were all under enormous psychological pressure. I felt it even from my relatives, those unspoken words, 'Shouldn't she be doing something for the war effort?' I could not, of course, tell them what I was doing. There was no safety valve. Often I would be beset by guilt. There was this all-pervading thought that if I had seen things a little clearer, a little quicker, men and ships might have been saved. It wasn't only our side which affected me. I handled some of the little, personal touches from German command headquarters to their U-boats. There was the message of congratulations to a Bosun Müller of one of their submarines in the Atlantic: 'You have a new son', it said. But I knew that as a result of our earlier de-coding, Müller's U-boat had been sunk the day before with the loss of all hands. There was never any triumphalism when we succeeded in what we had to do. It wasn't something that got just to us at Bletchley.

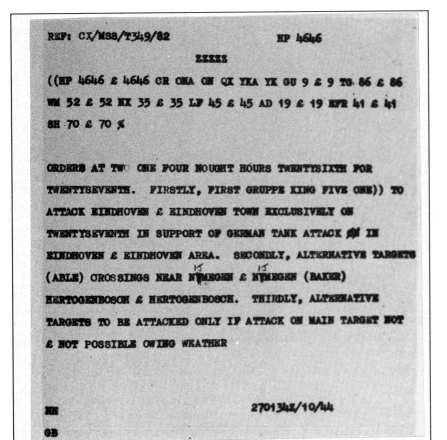

REF: CX/MSS/T349/82   HP 4646

ZZZZZ

((HP 4646 £ 4646 CR OMA OH QX YKA YK GU 9 £ 9 TO 86 £ 86

WM 52 £ 52 NX 35 £ 35 LP 45 £ 45 AD 19 £ 19 EFR 41 £ 41

SH 70 £ 70 %

ORDERS AT TWO ONE FOUR NOUGHT HOURS TWENTYSIXTH FOR

TWENTYSEVENTH. FIRSTLY, FIRST GRUPPE KING FIVE ONE)) TO

ATTACK EINDHOVEN £ EINDHOVEN TOWN EXCLUSIVELY ON

TWENTYSEVENTH IN SUPPORT OF GERMAN TANK ATTACK ØM IN

EINDHOVEN £ EINDHOVEN AREA. SECONDLY, ALTERNATIVE TARGETS

(ABLE) CROSSINGS NEAR NYMEGEN £ NYMEGEN (BAKER)

HERTOGENBOSCH £ HERTOGENBOSCH. THIRDLY, ALTERNATIVE

TARGETS TO BE ATTACKED ONLY IF ATTACK ON MAIN TARGET NOT

£ NOT POSSIBLE OWING WEATHER

NN   2701342/10/44

GB

A Bletchley Park signal to overseas commands giving German bombing intentions for the next day.

Crown Copyright. Reproduced with the permission of the Controller of Her Majesty's Stationery Office.

Edward Murch had been a coder aboard the *Prince of Wales*, together with the *Hood*, when they encountered the *Bismarck*. After the war, he retired to live on Dartmoor, where he writes poetry:

May the Twenty-Fourth*

That morning off Greenland seems an aeon away,
And the action we fought a lost glow in the dark;
But when memory stirs by the lake every May,
In the honk of the geese I hear *Bismarck, Bismarck*.

---

* 24 May 1941 was the day *Bismarck* sank HMS *Hood* with the loss of all but three of her 1,419 crew. The Royal Navy avenged the loss of the *Hood* on 27 May 1941 when they sank the *Bismarck* with the loss of over 2,000 of her crew.

Atlantic convoys could cover
hundreds of sea miles.

In 1942, the Germans introduced a new code called Triton, which put Bletchley back in the dark for a year. By 1943, the situation at sea had changed somewhat. American shipyards were building ships quicker than the Germans could sink them. They produced three Liberty ships a day. In November 1942, the *Robert E. Peary* was built and launched in just four days and 15 hours. The long-range B-24 Liberator became available to fill the Atlantic gap between Great Britain and the American east coast. It could stay in the air for 18 hours, thereby forcing the submarines to stay down. Submarine speed was only 7.5 knots submerged, insufficient even to catch the most decrepit of colliers. A further development was the escort carrier, a converted merchantman, often a Liberty ship, which provided convoys with air cover. There had also been a significant improvement in the numbers of destroyers and corvettes coming out of the shipyards and onto escort duties. Finally, the navy abandoned its compromised signals book, adopting a cypher system similar to Enigma. In the period March to May 1943, the Allies suffered heavy losses at the outset, but the sheer breadth and strength of their anti-submarine capabilities demonstrated their potential when, in May, they sank 43 U-boats. These were losses Dönitz could not bear and he called off the Battle of the Atlantic. He had lost 696 of the 830 submarines that were sent out on operations. In manpower terms, 25,870 of the total of 40,900 submariners never returned. A German authority on the Atlantic War was quite clear what the deciding influence was in relation to the timing of the celebration of victory:

Opposite: As the Battle of the Atlantic progressed, the hunters became the hunted. The U-boats were attacked from the sea . . .

. . . . and from the air. A German Type 7 U-boat under attack in the Atlantic.

I am sure that without the work of many unknown experts at Bletchley Park . . . the turning point of the Battle of the Atlantic would not have come as it did in May 1943, but months, perhaps many months, later. In that case the Allied invasion of Normandy would not have been possible in June 1944, and there would have ensued a chain of developments very different from the one which we have experienced.

THE HOME FRONT

'It so happens that this war, whether those at present in authority like it or not, has to be fought as a citizens' war', wrote J B Priestley in *Out of the People*.

There is no way out of that because in order to defend and protect this island, not only against possible invasion but also against all disasters of aerial bombardment, it has been found necessary to bring into existence a new network of voluntary associations such as the Home Guard, the Observer Corps, all the ARP and fire-fighting services and the like. They are a new type, what might be called the organised militant citizen.

What the war would do would be to make these ordinary people shareholders in the victory. Once achieved, they would expect their dividend in a Britain which Priestley described as 'being bombed and burned into democracy'.

Part of the clearing of decks for action involved the initiation of plans drawn up in 1938 for the evacuation of families and children from the designated vulnerable areas. In the three months up to 3 September 1939, over three and a half million people were moved from vulnerable areas to safer ones. Although the movements of evacuees in September involved over a quarter of the population, the voluntary evacuation plan fell well short of its potential. Less than half of London's schoolchildren left home and, in parts of the Midlands, the figures were in the region of 20 per cent. Prior to the move, billeting officers had gone out into the country to survey homes in order to identify the spare capacity to accommodate what were, in effect, the young representatives of the poorest elements of

Children collected in family groups before moving on to the designated railway station.

British society. At the appointed time, the bewildered children assembled in the railway stations of their cities, accompanied by a parent who would either be joining them, or be there to bid them a heart-wrenching farewell. As a general rule, mothers accompanied pre-school-aged children while schoolchildren were unaccompanied. The battalions of schoolchildren, each labelled with his or her name and destination, carrying a cardboard respirator box over the shoulder, and a parcel or suitcase of clothes, were sub-divided and led onto their designated platform for departure.

The arrival of these waifs into well-to-do areas of the countryside had a profound effect upon hosts and hostesses. They found it unimaginable that people of their own nationality should be existing in such indescribable circumstances. It was not so much their appalling clothing, the head lice, the bed-wetting and skin disease that opened eyes, but the children's behaviour. Underclothes were not at all common, lavatory paper was something entirely new to many, their language shocked the genteel, as did the discovery that some of these mites were accustomed to having a tipple. The children were little different from their parents. There is a comment in a 1950 HMSO report of an evacuated Glasgow mother chastising her six year old daughter for peeing upon their hostess's carpet: 'You dirty thing, messing up the lady's carpet. Go and do it in the corner'.

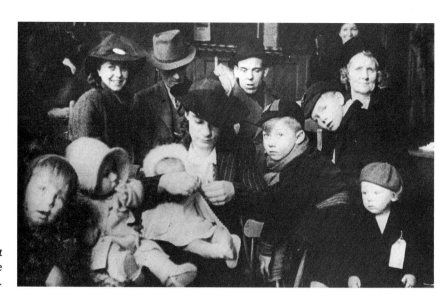

The mood was sombre but some attempted to put a brave face upon evacuation.

The hosts were compensated for taking in the evacuee children at the rate for full board of ten shillings and sixpence for the first child and eight shillings and sixpence for subsequent children. This amount was a useful sum in agricultural cottages but, in typical middle-class homes used to providing meals and accommodation to a higher standard, it was inadequate.

With the platform gate shut and the whistle having blown, these faces tell their own stories of grief.

A not untypical village of agricultural and middle-class homes was the 1939 Powerstock, lying four miles north-east of Bridport in Dorset. Terraces of stone cottages rise up out of the valley to the Norman Church of Saint Mary the Virgin on the upper terrace. It was in the vicarage here that the young Montgomery spent his holidays while his parents were abroad. Half way up the hill is the village church school and to the rear of it is an army hut of First World War vintage (still in use today for village activities). The Hut was brought into service as additional classrooms for the influx of the 100 schoolchildren evacuees. The school's capacity was only 70 to 80 pupils. It had been intended that the national school-leaving age would be raised from 14 to 15 on 1 September 1939 but it proved expedient to postpone this measure for eight years.

Powerstock was an agricultural village, yet one closely associated with the rope industry in Bridport. Women under 40 were not allowed to do nothing. They had to take part in essential war work. There was therefore a cottage industry of braiding nets, including camouflage nets and making up pull-throughs for guns. Each person so employed had a quota of one camouflage net a week. They were

Wartime Powerstock near Bridport, Dorset. Source: Private.

an industrious community, watched over by the lady at the manor, Mrs Crutchley, who toured the village in one of its few privately-owned cars. Petrol rationing restricted her to local journeys. She distributed petrol coupons and was also involved in the WVS. (Her husband, Captain Victor Crutchley VC RN, had been captain of the Jutland veteran HMS *Warspite* at Narvik, April 1940.) But in wartime the villagers were relatively comfortably off. Eggs, butter and cream were always available from one farmer or another. They grew their own vegetables and fruit and were allowed to keep half the livestock they raised for food.

September 1939 was a balmy month. The city children lost themselves in the folds of the hills and sunken lanes leading up to King John's Castle or high Eggardon Hill. They had not seen blackberries before and ate them voraciously. Here in these peaceful hills they had enormous freedom to live out their lives without fear. They needed no reminding that a war was on because there was a small garrison at the Manor House, and anti-aircraft guns had been deployed on the hills behind the village to intercept German bombers en route to the Midlands.

'Bubbles' Gray, who lives in one of the terraced houses on the road out to Poorton, was among those who took in evacuees. Her group, unusually, comprised three adults and one child from Plumstead. They got on famously and, after the war, the evacuees came back and spent their holidays with her. All the while, the government maintained an active propaganda programme for the evacuees to persevere and remain in the countryside, yet homesickness and pining were forces which could not be overcome and gradually the drift home began. By the beginning of 1940, 40 per cent of schoolchildren and 90 per cent of mothers with children under five had returned to their homes in the danger zones.

The women made the most of bringing up their families in those environments with which they were familiar. This phenomenon is often cited today as an example that single parenthood worked then and therefore should not be a social issue now. The circumstances were entirely different, for one important reason. Although the father was not at home, he was still tied to the home. Mothers recount how their greatest weapon in the armoury of discipline was the ultimate threat, 'just wait until your Dad gets home!'

As the weeks went by without bombs falling at home many evacuees returned to the cities, but when the Blitz began new evacuees arrived. The sophistication of this new group of children dumbfounded the village people. The bomb dropped on nearby West Milton was immediately dismissed as of little consequence by the East Enders who had faced intensive bombing each day. They would hold the locals in transfixed awe as they recounted their tales over kitchen tables. This went some way to offsetting their foreign habits.

An ARP (Air Raid Precautions) office.

At its outset, the Home Guard had an image problem. The principal reason for their formation was to intercept and disarm enemy parachutists. This picture was taken on 14 October 1940 and shows Doncaster's 5th Home Guard Battalion practising the searching of an enemy parachutist for arms.

The villagers had been instructed to be kind to their involuntary guests. Some found that to be extraordinarily difficult. There was a second evacuation from London when the city was hit by the V-1s and V-2s, as recounted on pp 91–97.

Powerstock's civil protection organisations were a microcosm of those which existed in the cities. The ARP (Air Raid Precautions) officers were located in a small room in the vicarage. During the period of the phoney war, the ARP were not taken at all seriously and their perceived officiousness caused intense irritation and aggravation among the community they served. Dubbed the " 'Anging Round Pubs", they came into their own, growing in stature once the bombing really started. A post would be manned by half a dozen wardens for every 400 to 500 people in urban areas. In May 1941, they became uniformed with blue serge overcoats, berets, boots and badges of rank. There was often conflict with the self-important Home Guard and, in that respect, the aggravation represented between Mr Hodges and Mr Mainwaring in *Dad's Army* was close to the truth. ARP male volunteers were over 30 and women over 25. Their role was to identify and report all aircraft sightings and bombings [the tracking of enemy aircraft within the radar net was that of the Royal Observer Corps], to enforce the blackout, to notify the presence of poison gas, and to deal with the calling out of the emergency services and the calming of the public. In 1938, the ARP had a women's section known as the Women's Voluntary Service (WVS) but once war started, the WVS took on a number of varied roles, the nature of which could be summarised by their motto: 'If it should be done, the WVS will do it'.

The fear of German parachutists and the work of a 'Fifth Column' in Great Britain prompted Secretary for War, Anthony Eden, to broadcast to the nation on 14 May 1940. He called for men between the ages of 17 and 65 to join the Local Defence Volunteers (LDV). Overnight, queues formed outside police stations, of citizens keen to do their bit. In a matter of six weeks, a million and a half men had signed up for what, in July, Churchill would redesignate the Home Guard. One grammar schoolboy of the time remembers the shock and delight which ran through the morning assembly when the headmaster, a former regular infantry officer, marched on to the stage wearing brown boots, breeches, khaki jacket, gown and LDV armband and announced that he had been appointed Commanding Officer of the town's defences.

Beaminster District 440 Mounted Home Guard Unit with commanding officer Dr Arnold Lake. They held their annual camps with similar units from Dorchester and Maiden Newton at the army camp in Piddletrenthide.
(Private)

Powerstock raised three sections. The zeal of two of those sections gave their fellow villagers cause to ponder whether they feared the Home Guard more than the threat posed by German parachutists. To them, it was as though they were Boy Scouts with shotguns. Rifles were not immediately available, so the men took out their own weapons, which were essentially shotguns. They would establish road blocks at the drop of a hat to check identities, to ensure that there were no German sympathisers passing through the village. The third section was more laid back – literally so. They often went out at night and returned in the morning, having spent the evening asleep in the hedgerows. There was also a District Mounted Home Guard, made up of a score of local farmers and grooms whose role was to run messages and to provide communications across country which they knew like the backs of their hands.

In time, the Home Guard's efficiency increased so that they were able to take over important duties, releasing the regular army for D-Day preparations.

The Home Guard suffered a major image problem. So much equipment had been lost at Dunkirk that all resources were concentrated upon the refurbishment of the army proper. The hopes that had run so high on that heady day in May were soon dashed when the volunteers discovered the only item of uniform they had in common was an armband which proclaimed the wearer to be a member of the Local Defence Volunteers. Many of those who had come forward, took advantage of the 'two weeks' notice and out' before voting with their feet, leaving a small hardcore of those prepared to train and drill regularly. Gradually the lot of the Home Guard improved when uniforms and equipment came on stream. The government took a more positive attitude towards the volunteers, backing it with new legislation. In November 1942, conscription of men aged 18 to 51 enabled commanding officers to fill the gaps which had appeared in their ranks. Moreover, fines were levied against those men who did not attend drill nights. No longer could men leave the Home Guard after giving two weeks' notice. Ironically, as the Home Guard's professionalism increased, so the likely need to employ them decreased. In March 1943 they had become a 1,800,000-strong force of some consequence, very often with real wartime roles. For example, their taking over the function of coastal observation from regulars, released the latter for the specialist training they would require for the coming D-Day. It was the success of D-Day which spelt the demise of the Home Guard. Soon after the initial victories in France had been consolidated, the Home Front was no longer at risk from a German invasion. On 3 December 1944, the Home Guard was stood down, a further milestone in the road towards victory in Europe.

At the beginning of the war the Red Cross and Saint John's Ambulance Brigade were combined into a Joint War Organisation. Over 90,000 worked closely with the Civil Defence, while others raised funds to send books and food parcels to Prisoners of War. The Fire Services began precautionary recruiting in 1938. In addition, an Auxiliary Fire Service was created, attracting those too old or too infirm for military service. The Fire Brigades had been organised previously on a local basis and were accountable to the local authorities. Operations and equipment were not standardised, and it was not until 1941 that this nettle was grasped. The 1,400 separate

The Fire Services throughout the towns and cities of the land gave heroic service. These firemen are at work in Eastcheap, London.

services went into the melting pot, out of which emerged 39 units in a new National Fire Service. It was dangerous work. Individuals in a number of Fire Brigades, particularly those in London, were at greater risk to loss of life and limb than were individual soldiers.

Country villages such as Powerstock were subjected to further expansion in their population when volunteers arrived to help with the harvest. Government posters, aimed at those with time on their hands, announced pointedly: 'You are needed in the fields' and 'Come and help with the victory harvest'. Schools also sent large numbers of boys and girls to harvest camps. The men had largely been withdrawn from the fields for priority service elsewhere. Their places were taken by an 80,000-strong Women's Land Army, but not without a great deal of residual prejudice. These women worked a 50-hour week, for which they were paid £1-8s-6d (£1-42½). More specifically, there was also the kitchen propaganda exhorting people to 'dig for victory', as well as advice to housewives on how to make nourishing food from dull and unusual ingredients. When the harvest had been safely gathered in, the Ministry of Information would introduce a new campaign, 'Come into the factories'.

Powerstock's school bell was taken away early in the war to be melted down into a piece of war-winning equipment. Lord Beaverbrook, the controversial Minister of Air Production, appealed to housewives to hand in their aluminium saucepans to be turned into Spitfires. It was a good idea in theory, but the aluminium content of many of the saucepans was too low to be of use and consequently, throughout the country, there were strategic piles of unwanted cooking pans. What Lord Beaverbrook did was to re-organise the industry's work practice to ensure that Spitfires were coming on stream when most needed. Prior to Beaverbrook's appointment, the monthly budget for the production of Spitfires was 250–260. In May 1940, 261 Spitfires were expected, but 325 were produced. Deliveries continued to increase; 446 in June, 496 in July, from which point production settled at over 100 above April's target. British industry made prodigious progress to upgrade its work capacity and thereby make up the many shortfalls in the Services' inventories. 'The production which you pour out of your factories

Members of the Women's Land Army at work.

There were always jobs in the factories to keep hands busy.

this week', Lord Beaverbrook told aircraft workers, 'will be hurled into the desperate struggle next week'. When raw material production – such as in the coalfields – fell below target, one tenth of 1943 conscripts were sent down the pits or volunteered to go. They were known as Bevin Boys after Ernest Bevin, the Minister of Labour; some of them subsequently registered as conscientious objectors when they had to leave the pits.

There was nothing quite like the Blitz to act so successfully to bond most men in the street with the men in uniform as partners in a dreadful war. When an American radio reporter visited London to gain a first-hand account of the civilians' experience of the German bombing campaign, he was told very firmly 'there are no civilians here'. It had all begun on a beautiful September summer's day, the weather reminiscent of the year before. The Blitz started over London at 5pm on Saturday, 7 September 1940 and continued for 76 nights, except for 2 November, without interruption. On that fateful September night, fire-watchers close to Wren's masterpiece, St Paul's Cathedral, watched in awe and horror as the incendiaries and high explosives generated and spawned the spreading fires. 'It's like the end of the world', said one. To which another replied, 'it *is* the end of the world'. The bombers swarmed around London like bees round a honey pot. Its attraction as the nation's capital, seat of government and commercial centre was all pervading. Unlike some midland cities which had the space to build dummy, replica cities beyond the real city boundaries, London could enjoy no such possibility. That trusty, faithful servant, Old Father Thames, did London no favours as its silvery finger pointed into the very heart of the capital. German direction guidance systems had no difficulty in targeting bombers on London. Moreover, RAF night-fighters and anti-aircraft guns proved to be almost ineffective in stopping the nightly procession of bombers over the city. On 11 September, Fighter Command lost 29 aircraft to the Luftwaffe's 24. The ratio changed to the RAF's advantage, particularly when the Germans mounted daylight attacks.

A Heinkel He III above Greenwich.

A German land mine collapsed the Bank underground station and destroyed the whole square. The Mansion House is in the background.

Within a fortnight, a quarter of the residents of Bermondsey, Deptford, Stepney, Poplar and Shoreditch had been bombed out or had moved out of the area. Nor was the central part of the city spared. For example, it had been estimated that by November, every acre of Holborn had been hit by approximately 20 tons of high explosive. Churchill trudged through the streets and over the wreckage that had once been people's homes. 'Are we downhearted?', he shouted. To which they responded with good, firm voices, 'No!' A wife who had recently taken up a nursing job, wrote to her Service husband from Clarges Street W1 on 10 September.

The last three nights have been absolute hell. We are bombed from about 8.30pm to 5.30am every night and I have not had more than two or three hours sleep on either night. I sleep in the afternoon whenever I can but, would just give anything for a quiet night in the country, but I have taken up this job and cannot back out of it now on account of danger . . . They say now that all leave is stopped as an invasion is expected. *It really is just my luck* for this to start when I get comfortably settled with a job here.

On 13 September, a raider bombed Buckingham Palace. The King and Queen had remained in London among their people. This bombing and two others which followed, emphasised the struggle of one unified nation. The Queen said, in a matter of fact way, 'I am glad we have been bombed. It makes me feel I can look the East End in the face'.

The pre-occupation with, and publicity given to London during the Blitz caused some jealousy and annoyance in other cities in the

London's tightly packed terraced housing was especially vulnerable to enemy bombing.

land. However, the statistics for 1940–1941 reveal that 60 per cent of the houses destroyed and 50 per cent of those killed, lived in London. In Central London, only one house in ten escaped damage. 43,000 civilians died over that period compared with 17,000 between 1942–1945. In fact, during the period 1939–1942, the enemy had killed more women and children than soldiers. It is not surprising, therefore, that when the time to celebrate victory arrived, it was celebrated in London more lavishly, on a greater scale and with greater relief and enthusiasm than anywhere else.

Opposite: Londoners taking overnight shelter at the Elephant and Castle underground station. Only four per cent of Londoners took shelter in the underground system.

27 per cent of Londoners took shelter in Anderson shelters. As is evident from this scene in Lewisham, they were sturdy enough to survive all but a direct hit.

A gutted dwelling. A sign tells passers by to keep their hands off. In wartime Great Britain, looting could be punished by death or lifetime imprisonment.

It has always been assumed that when the sirens sounded at night, London's population went to ground in London Underground stations, in public shelters, or small six-man shelters dug-in in back gardens and named Anderson shelters after Chamberlain's Home Secretary, Sir John Anderson. These were provided free for many people but the middle classes had to pay for their own – a strange inversion of privilege as many of the better off did not bother. The London Transport Authority, encouraged by the government who had no wish to cultivate a subterranean society, refused the Londoners access to their underground platforms. The sheer numbers who were not going to be dictated to, had their way, and London Transport and the Government relented with good grace. In September 1940, the tube system was accommodating 177,000. A November 1940 survey showed four per cent of London's population to be sheltering at night in the underground system, another nine per cent took refuge in public shelters, and 27 per cent in Anderson shelters. This meant that 60 per cent of London's population were not taking serious shelter precautions at all. Some would make the concession of taking cover under a stout table by a window, or under the stairs, but many took an extraordinarily philosophical view: 'If your number's on it, your time's up'.

The Londoners' humour was severely tested in the first two weeks in September, when it was so obviously apparent that the emergency services were totally unprepared for the scale of damage inflicted upon London. Communists did emerge to make political capital, but with little real success. The losses were far less than predicted and Germany did not have sufficient bombers to damage London's indomitable spirit. Many of those living in London had declined to be evacuated to safer areas. To some extent, therefore, their stoicism derived from the fact that they were in London voluntarily. There were other centres of production and other ports to which Germany turned her attention in November 1940.

Coventry in 1940 was a small, compact, industrial city of approximately a quarter of a million inhabitants. Its importance lay in the nature of its industries, associated as they were with motor and aircraft production. The commotion and sheer panic caused when the Germans bombed the city on 14 November 1940 exceeded anything that had been seen in London. Four hundred bombers had succeeded in destroying three quarters of Coventry city centre, including inflicting serious damage on 21 strategically important factories as well as public utilities. Five hundred people were killed in the raid, less than had been killed aboard HMS *Courageous* and a little over one third of those killed aboard HMS *Hood*. Coventry, on the other hand, had been shaken to its roots and the levels of distress had reached such high proportions as to threaten to overflow into neighbouring communities. The Luftwaffe's tactics were open to criticism. Rather than launch a follow-up attack the next day, they resumed their bombing of the by now blasé Londoners. What Coventry demonstrated was a preparedness of the Luftwaffe to venture out to strike strategic provincial centres such as Southampton, Plymouth, Liverpool, the Clyde, the Midlands, Hull and Glasgow among others.

The final phase of the London Blitz took place between 16 April – 10 May 1941 with mass attacks involving 500-700 bombers. On 10 May, the Luftwaffe attacked across a broad band from Hammersmith out to Essex, killing 1,436 people. That was the peak of the enemy's

Winston Churchill touring the ruins of Coventry Cathedral.

No matter how badly British cities suffered, German cities suffered worse. This is an aerial view of the damage to Cologne after an Allied bombing raid in 1945.

air activity over London, during which they dropped over 12,000 tons of bombs. Luftwaffe squadrons in the west were re-located in the east, to take the battle into Russia. The cities of Britain had suffered badly, but the people's spirit remained supremely defiant in the face of saturation bombing. They proved that 'London can take it'. Either that lesson had not been learnt by the RAF or they considered the German civilians to be made of lesser stuff when they launched their own strategic bombing campaign against Germany. The debate as to the merit or needs of the RAF's bombing campaign will continue. As many of Hamburg's residents were killed as in the whole of Great Britain, while Dresden suffered almost three times as many. It was as a result of an RAF raid on the historic Baltic port of Lübeck that Hitler ordered the so-called Baedeker retaliatory raids.

The Baedeker raids were named after the famous tour guides and reflected the rationale of this type of raid. They were targeted against famous English historic towns, well-known for their mediaeval or

Georgian architecture. The raids were not conducted by large numbers of bombers but were an extension of the 'tip and run' type bombing raids which had become a feature of action against the south and east coasts. One of the reasons for their effectiveness, as well as their notoriety, was the fact that the selected towns were initially totally unprepared. The first Baedeker raid was launched against Exeter on 24 April 1942 and they continued for two months with attacks, some multiple, against Bath, Norwich, York and Canterbury. The 'tip and run' bombing sorties went on for another year. They were never to reach the levels of intensity of the bombing campaign of the Blitz but they were sufficient to cause a continuing loss of life, intense irritation and substantial loss of production.

The amazing feature of D-Day was not so much the brilliance of its logistics or the imagination of the deception planning, which resulted in only 18 of the available 60 German divisions facing the Allied landings, but rather that so many men, machines and equipment could have been assembled for so long without their intentions being realised. In common with so many routes, the length of

D-Day, 6 June 1944. 48 Royal Marine Commando going ashore on Nan Red Beach, Juno Area, St. Aubyn sur Mer.

'. . . and saw a shape with a fiery tail rushing past my window . . .'

Watling Street* was congested with military vehicles pointing south, a million and a half foreign servicemen had been encamped in the southern counties for months and, out at sea, there gathered a great armada of warships, landing craft and prefabricated docks. That this was at all possible was due to the defeat of the Luftwaffe, an air force whose forays over Great Britain were now so few and far between that the threat of aerial bombing had all but disappeared. D-Day was 6 June and, by midnight, 156,000 men were ashore in France. This, coupled with the Soviet advances in the East, was the beginning of the end of the Third Reich. There was no further, compelling, strategic merit in bombing London and the other British cities away from the south coast. But it had been the British who had been Hitler's ulcer, niggling away at him until it grew and became a major factor in his downfall. The Allied intelligence services had known for over a year of the German development of long-range, pilotless weapons. In June, the V-1 bases in France were ready to launch Hitler's revenge or 'vengeance' weapons on Great Britain. (The 'V' stood for *Vergeltungswaffe*, meaning retaliatory weapon.)

The first noticeable evidence of the pilotless planes was on 15 June 1944 and the next day, the 16th, the government told the public to prepare for attack by what would be described as 'flying bombs'. One

---

* A Roman road running north-west across England from Richborough in Kent through London and St Albans to Wroxeter in Shropshire.

of the very first flying bombs came down on the evening of 16 June at 9.35pm in Caldbeck Avenue, Worcester Park, South London. The damage was extensive and at least 10 people were killed. Parallel to Caldbeck Avenue runs Longfellow Road, the home of Mr and Mrs Major-Ball. The Major-Balls' elder son was in hospital with scarlet fever but, at 9.30pm, his younger brother John was asleep in his cot in the front room. His mother entered the room, picked up the baby, and went out into the hall. It was at this point that the bomb fell. The front room window had been blown in and shards of jagged glass speared the empty cot of the man who would later become Prime Minister.

The diary of a London woman reveals how the unwelcome phenomenon of flying bombs was received. Her entry for 17 June reads as follows:

We were warned by the BBC that a pilotless plane had been launched over the Southern Counties. Saw my first one on June 17th, when spending night at Annies Cottage, Rusper, Sussex. Slept in little bedroom overlooking the church. The Home Guard patrolled outside all night watching for the new planes. Heard awful rattling noise in early hours of morning and

Bofors guns deployed to the coast to intercept incoming V-1 flying bombs.

'So long as it "buzzed", they were safe; when its engine cut out, someone was in trouble.' In this case, the V-1 fell in a side road off Drury Lane.

saw a shape with a fiery tail rushing past my window . . . returned home on June 17th via Croydon and bicycled from Croydon via Monk's Orchard. Nearly everyone wearing tin hats to ward off shrapnel.

And the next day, the 18th:

The RAF have nicknamed the bombs 'Doodlebugs' and this name has caught on with the public. Some call them buzzbombs and some say robot or flying bombs. They are nasty things – dropping chiefly on Croydon and the boroughs south of the Thames. It is a comparative rest cure to go up to Central London . . . In Catford I have heard 4-6 bombs fell in a space of ten minutes several times.

The Germans must have realised that it was just a matter of time before the V-1 bases were located and destroyed, hence their frenetic activity in getting the maximum number into the air in the shortest possible time. Their sites in northern France were overrun by the forces of liberation in August 1944. In the space of a fortnight, they managed to put 100 V-1s a day into the air. At the other side of the Channel there were the combined forces of the Royal Air Force and

Three minutes after a V-1 hit a row of shops in Clapham Junction, London, 17 June 1944.

Anti-Aircraft Command to field them. A good proportion of London's guns were moved out to the coast. The problem with V-1 bombs that were tipped off course by RAF fighters or were damaged by ack-ack guns was that they exploded on landing. The civilians in greater London grew accustomed to picking up the buzzing sound of the closing bombs. So long as it 'buzzed', they were safe; when its engine cut out, someone was in trouble. As the diarist above asserted, the London borough of Croydon's experience of flying bombs was equal to anything experienced at the height of the Blitz. A second evacuation had begun. One hundred and forty two bombs fell within the borough boundary causing a substantial number of casualties and much blast damage to property. A single bomb's capacity to kill, maim and destroy was enormous. One which fell on the Guards' Chapel in West London on 18 June during the course of a military service, killed 119; 102 were seriously injured. The high proportion of death to injury was not at all unusual. The onslaught lasted for 80 days, but the law of reducing return prevailed. In all, 6,000 civilians were killed and 16,000 badly injured. The preventive measures were beefed up, employing more aircraft and thickening the air defences on the coast. The Germans then resorted to the launching of V-1s from aircraft. Although this ploy was infrequent, it did serve to widen the area over which the bombs fell. Twenty seven people were killed in Oldham, Lancashire on 24 December 1944. The main thrust of the V-1 had been defeated, but on 8 September the peace of London was shattered by two explosions of unknown origin.

Not wishing to panic the people, the government attributed the mysterious explosions in their midst to explosions of gas. The public wondered why it was that, until recently, there had been no town gas explosions and now, suddenly, they were experiencing up to six

This old man left his wife cooking Sunday lunch while he took the dog for a walk. The V-1 hit his home while he was away, killing his wife.

a day. They could see the incoming rockets quite distinctly from their fiery tails; they called them 'flying gas mains'. There was no press comment, for they had been gagged by the government. It was not until 10 November 1944 that Churchill admitted in the House of Commons that London was being subjected to rocket attacks. He

A V-2 being prepared for lift-off.

hoped to ease the people's fear of the unknown by emphasising that the rockets were not effective as overall weapons of destruction. Certainly they did not adversely affect the morale of a philosophical people who were absolutely convinced of the logic of 'if your number's on it'. There would be a bang and the people in the vicinity would be dead, alive, or alive but injured. Individually, the V-2 rocket bombs were highly destructive, as well as immune to interception. Four landed on Croydon, collectively damaging 2,000 houses and thereby adding to the city's burgeoning housing problem.

There is a common belief that the V-2s were engaged exclusively against Great Britain from Peenemünde in northern Germany. The first operational V-2 launched by the Germans was launched from Belgium against Paris on 5 September 1944. The first rockets to land in London were launched from Holland. Antwerp in Belgium was hit by 1,265 V-2s, while London was hit by 518. Fixed sites were built, but were destroyed before they could become operational. All the V-2s were launched by mobile units, from sites adapted for the purpose. Thus, they proved enormously difficult to detect and were progressively overrun by the advancing Allied troops. The last V-2 to fall on England fell on Orpington on 27 March 1945. The number of people killed by V-2s totalled 2,724, and over 6,000 were seriously injured.

In comparison to what had gone before, the V-1s and V-2s had not had a major impact upon the blitzed, war-weary people of Britain. Provided morale remained high, as it did, the killing had no more strategic point than did the Allied bombing of German cities in 1945. One overwhelming reason for this was that the Allied war machines, the massive power of the Soviet, American and British armies and air forces ground on relentlessly, despite the V-weapons. They may sometimes have advanced slowly, with halts such as the Russian political pause in Poland from August 1944 to January 1945, and setbacks like the Battle of the Bulge in December 1944 and January 1945, but there were also spurts, like the race across France in August 1944. In this way, the Allies closed in remorselessly and inevitably on the last strongholds of the Third Reich. In the Far East too the tide had turned in Burma and the Philippines.

In Western Europe the D-Day invasion succeeded although not without many casualties and hard battles, of which Omaha Beach and

The inhabitants of Brussels greet British and Belgian troops after the liberation of the city, 3 September 1944. Antwerp fell to the British the following day.

Russian and American soldiers rest on the banks of the Elbe following the link-up between the US 1st Army and the Russian 1st Ukrainian Army at Torgau, 60 miles south of Berlin, 25 April 1945.

Caen were examples. Italy had, of course, already surrendered although much of it was still under German occupation. Southern France was invaded in August 1944. The Allies broke out of the Normandy beachhead and between 7 August and 4 September France was liberated, General Leclerc of the Free French Forces entering Paris on 25 August. On 1 September, Monty handed over command of the land forces to General Eisenhower, thus recognising the superior size of the US war effort. Brussels was liberated by the British on 3 September, followed by Antwerp the next day. The advance continued but got stuck in the Netherlands in September, a pause which Arnhem failed to cure. In the winter, Hitler made a desperate attempt to stem the tide in the Ardennes but his counter-attack inevitably petered out. In March, the Rhine was crossed and the advance into Germany began on a broad front. Meanwhile in the East, the Russian advance began again in the North in January while by mid-April, Stalin had conquered Central Europe from Prague to Trieste. The Russian armies closed on Berlin; on 25 April, the Russian 58th Guards Division linked up with the US 273rd Regiment at Torgau on the Elbe; on 30 April, Hitler shot himself and on 2 May what remained of the Berlin garrison, and also the German forces in Italy, surrendered.

All this was heady stuff on the Home Front and the people shrugged off the technologically advanced but futile threat of the V-weapons.

The scene was set for Victory and V-E Day.

CELEBRATION OF VICTORY

When V-E Day arrived, it did not come with neat military precision but as a clumsy stop-go affair, brought about by a newsman's betrayal of confidence and the need to collaborate the announcement with the Soviets. It was clear in April 1945 that V-E Day was imminent, but what was not clear was precisely when. As has already been portrayed, the Germans were cracking under the strain imposed by two converging armies. The German military tried desperately to surrender to the west while Stalin ordered his two principal commanders to be the first to enter and win Berlin. Hitler married his mistress, Eva Braun, in his Berlin bunker before poisoning her and his dog on 30 April. He then took his own life. The next day, May Day, German radio announced the death of the Führer. The announcer said Hitler had been killed in the Battle of Berlin and added that the Commander-in-Chief of the German Navy, Admiral Karl Dönitz, architect of the Battle of the Atlantic, was appointed Hitler's successor. This was Dönitz's reward for loyalty to the Führer.

Dönitz established the new seat of government in Flensburg, about as far north as it is possible to go in Germany without crossing into Denmark. This part of northern Germany also happened to be the operational area of Field Marshal Montgomery's 21st Army Group. There was no distinct front line to facilitate a clear-cut cessation of hostilities. Understandably, Hamburg and Kiel were yet to fall, but there were still areas in the Netherlands in German hands, including Amsterdam and Rotterdam. Montgomery's superior, General Eisenhower, had his Supreme Headquarters, Allied Expeditionary Force (SHAEF) 400 miles to the southwest of 21st Army Group in Rheims, in the heart of France's Champagne district.

Such a degree of separation gave Montgomery much satisfaction, particularly when it put him, and by association the British, in the spotlight for managing the surrender of Germany's forces in the north.

Montgomery's Headquarters had been established out on Lüneburg Heath. It comprised a large grouping of marquees and caravans. It was here, at 11.30am on a blustery Thursday, 3 May, that a four man delegation acting on behalf of Admiral Dönitz arrived to discuss surrender terms. Dönitz had not come himself, but sent instead, as leader of the delegation, his own successor, the new Commander-in-Chief of the German Navy, Admiral von Friedeburg. Montgomery received the Germans under a flagpole flying the Union Jack. Their mission concerned not what was happening on the Western Front but rather what was happening on the Eastern Front. In short, they wanted to surrender to Montgomery three German Armies withdrawing in front of the Russians between Berlin and Rostock and to protect the German

The meeting on Lüneburg Heath between Field Marshal Montgomery and the German delegation led by Admiral von Friedeburg, 3 May 1945.

Field Marshal Montgomery reading the Instrument of Surrender to the German delegation.

civilian population in Mecklenburg. Montgomery told them that what they asked was outside his jurisdiction. Von Friedeburg protested. He said the Russians were savages and he feared the German prisoners would be transported into the depths of Russia. 'I said the Germans should have thought of all these things before they began the war', wrote Montgomery, 'and particularly before they attacked the Russians in June 1941'. Thus the Germans had arrived not to surrender their forces facing 21st Army Group but troops engaged in fighting in and around Berlin. Montgomery insisted that von Friedeburg must surrender all German forces on the Western Front, otherwise he would order a continuation of the fighting. Von Friedeburg protested – he had no such authority to do as Montgomery wished. In his typically schoolmasterish manner, Montgomery told the German admiral to go back, seek the necessary authority, and return by six o'clock the next day. When the German delegation reassembled on 4 May, they duly signed the instrument of battlefield surrender. Arrangements were then made to fly the Germans to Rheims to sign a General Surrender.

The weather over western Europe on 5 May was particularly bad. Admiral von Friedeburg's plane, unable to land at Rheims, landed instead at Brussels, from where the delegation travelled on to Rheims

<u>Instrument of Surrender</u>

of

<u>All German armed forces in HOLLAND, in</u>

<u>northwest Germany including all islands,</u>

<u>and in DENMARK.</u>

1. The German Command agrees to the surrender of all German armed forces in HOLLAND, in northwest GERMANY including the FRISIAN ISLANDS and HELIGOLAND and all other islands, in SCHLESWIG-HOLSTEIN, and in DENMARK, to the C.-in-C. 21 Army Group. *This to include all naval ships in these areas.* These forces to lay down their arms and to surrender unconditionally.

2. All hostilities on land, on sea, or in the air by German forces in the above areas to cease at 0800 hrs. British Double Summer Time on Saturday 5 May 1945.

3. The German command to carry out at once, and without argument or comment, all further orders that will be issued by the Allied Powers on any subject.

4. Disobedience of orders, or failure to comply with them, will be regarded as a breach of these surrender terms and will be dealt with by the Allied Powers in accordance with the accepted laws and usages of war.

5. This instrument of surrender is independent of, without prejudice to, and will be superseded by any general instrument of surrender imposed by or on behalf of the Allied Powers and applicable to Germany and the German armed forces as a whole.

6. This instrument of surrender is written in English and in German.

    The English version is the authentic text.

7. The decision of the Allied Powers will be final if any doubt or dispute arises as to the meaning or interpretation of the surrender terms.

B. L. Montgomery
Field-Marshal

4 May 1945
1830 hrs

The Instrument of Surrender signed on 4 May 1945.

by road. During the course of a preliminary session, von Friedeburg revealed that he had only the authority to negotiate, not to surrender. By now, the free world's press had gathered at Rheims, eager to make the announcement that the war in Europe had ended. Meanwhile von Friedeburg, who found his role painful and humiliating (he later committed suicide), had no means of contacting Dönitz directly. The Americans insisted he must surrender unconditionally, nothing less than capitulation would do; something he could not do without Dönitz's authority. Von Friedeburg thereupon drafted a signal to be encoded and sent along a fractured chain of command to Dönitz in Flensburg. All this, of course, took time.

Sunday, 6 May was a day when the numbers of the press corps in Rheims had grown even larger; so large that a pool of 17 was selected to represent the world's press on the occasion of the signing of the peace. It was, however, a day of frustrating inactivity, that is until 6pm when Admiral Dönitz's emissary, the German Chief of Staff, General Alfred Jodl arrived. During the course of the evening, a number of conferences were convened, but it soon became apparent that the Germans were trying to postpone the awful moment of capitulation. Thereupon, General Eisenhower gave them a 48-hour

General Eisenhower making a V for Victory with the pens used for signing the unconditional surrender of Germany's armed forces at HQ SHAEF, Rheims, 7 May 1945. On the left is Lieutenant General Walter Bedell Smith, who presided, and on the right, Eisenhower's deputy, Air Chief Marshal Sir Arthur Tedder. Looking on is Eisenhower's personal staff officer, Kay Summersby.

ultimatum. Jodl recognised that the writing was well and truly on the wall and signalled Dönitz to the effect that, in his opinion, there was no alternative. It was a question, he suggested, of chaos or signature and, accordingly, he sought the authority to sign the document of capitulation. The necessary authorisations were in place for the document to be signed at 2.41am on Monday, 7 May 1945. The American General Bedell Smith presided. General Jodl signed on behalf of Admiral Dönitz and, for the Russians and French, Susloparov and Sevez appended their signatures. The Second World War was officially at an end. It had not ended as the First had, by the instrument of an armistice, but through the complete and unconditional surrender of German armed forces. It was at this point the procedural problems began.

Churchill, Roosevelt and Stalin had agreed earlier that the announcement of war's end would be made simultaneously in London, Washington and Moscow once the German surrender had been ratified in Berlin. This meant that the pool of reporters who had witnessed the German capitulation were effectively gagged until given the green light to proceed. The military staff at Rheims believed there to be absolutely no possibility that the story would not be leaked. Nevertheless, they went through the process of complying with their orders. On 7 May, SHAEF sent a secret signal to the liaison censors in Brussels.

> Negotiations have been completed for the surrender of the German Government and the German Armed Forces. The ceasefire will be effective 0001 DBST (Double British Summer Time) 9th May 1945. No publication of this fact will be permitted until an announcement is made by the Allied Chiefs of State. It is understood that this announcement will be made at 1500 hours DBST 8 May 1945.

The details of the surrender were transmitted to allied governments and other interested parties in code rather than in clear, and the pool reporters were denied access to military communication means.

There was one in the 'pool' who had the privileged information, who was determined that this scoop should not lie dormant, to await the enactment of some political nicety and the opening of the flood gates as other newsmen filed their copy. The villain of this particular piece, the first to announce the ending of the war, was Edward Kennedy, employed by the Associated Press Agency. Eisenhower was left furious and embarrassed, the other members of the 'pool' distressed at having been gazumped, and heavy clouds hung over London, Washington and Moscow. Kennedy knew that the German headquarters in Flensburg had already announced the surrender to their own men in the field – to tell them to stop fighting. Kennedy argued that the matter was no longer a secret and insisted that he should now be permitted to contact his agency. The censors demurred. No doubt steamed up with the old press chestnut of 'the public's right to know', Kennedy filed his story by telephone through to Associated Press's London office.

America had been hit by a false alarm before the end of April and was slow to react to Kennedy's scoop. However, once the momentum developed, there were scenes of great rejoicing and thanksgiving from New York across to San Francisco – that is, until SHAEF poured cold water upon the celebrations. Eisenhower's staff put out a press release to the effect that they had not announced the surrender of the German Armed Forces in Europe. They did not say that what Kennedy had reported was untrue, but rather left the public to assume that was the case. Reading between the lines, the astute recognised that the war had indeed ended, but it had not been officially declared. After all, the German Foreign Minister, Schwerin von Krosigk, had broadcast from Flensburg that 'after a heroic fight of almost six years of incomparable hardness, Germany has succumbed to the overwhelming power of her enemies'. The London papers on the morning of 7 May hedged their bets with non-commital headlines. Meanwhile, in London, the public had been out in the streets, wondering whether they should be celebrating or not. By tea-time, when nothing had been announced, they broke up disconsolately and headed homeward. This uncertainty clearly annoyed Churchill, who decided to set aside his pledge to Stalin. Accordingly, at 7.40pm, in a roundabout way, the Ministry of Information announced the end of the war:

It is understood that, in accordance with arrangements between the three great powers, an official announcement will be broadcast by the Prime Minister at three o'clock tomorrow, Tuesday afternoon, 8 May. In view of this fact, tomorrow, Tuesday, will be treated as Victory in Europe Day and will be regarded as a holiday. The day following, Wednesday, 9 May, will also be a holiday. His Majesty the King will broadcast to the people of the British Empire and Commonwealth, tomorrow, Tuesday, at 9pm.

A higher proportion of people than had been out in the streets during the day now crammed the centre of London in spontaneous celebration of what the morrow would bring. A crowd assembled around Big Ben cheered when the great bell struck 12. As midnight ushered in the long awaited day, ships as distant as Southampton and the Clyde, and tugs on the Thames, let out their assorted, raucous noises while bursts from searchlights shot like tracer into the depths of the dark sky their morse message of Victory.

Meanwhile, at Rheims, Eisenhower's deputy, Air Chief Marshal Sir Arthur Tedder, prepared with the American General Spaatz and

Eager soldiers pulling copies of 'Stars and Stripes' from the press of the London 'Times' at 9pm on 7 May 1945, when an extra edition was put out to announce the news of Germany's surrender.

French General de Lattre de Tassigny to fly to Berlin on 8 May to ratify the document of surrender with the Russians. The German delegation comprised Field Marshal Keitel, Admiral von Friedeburg and Air Marshal Stumpf.

Tedder took with him the Draft Instrument of Surrender which was broadly similar to the one signed at Rheims. Marshal Zhukov had not, of course, seen such a document before and was very much guided by a Deputy Commissar for Foreign Affairs by the name of Andrei Vyshinsky. Tedder records: 'I had a feeling that the presence or absence of M. Vyshinsky was a potent factor which determined the progress, or lack of it, in our negotiations'. The allies spent 12 hours arguing over the detail contained in the Draft Instrument of Surrender. The Russians even proposed one amendment which would have involved handing the Germans over to Russia. Eventually the allies signed the document before calling the Germans forward to do likewise. The Second World War was now truly over.

There was no standard response to the dawning of V-E Day. Individuals reacted differently according to their situation, experience and emotions.

There is, for example, the case of the Shepperds. Lesley Shepperd's father had been killed at Gallipoli when she was only three. She never knew a father: First World War widows had little prospect of remarrying – they were the involuntary recruits in the great regiments of surplus women. There were no men; they were dead. When Lesley married her soldier husband Alan, she had an abiding dread of war. Alan, a 33-year old Lieutenant Colonel in the Manchester Regiment, had been a well-known Army sportsman representing the Service in hockey and shooting. He went over to France on 7 July 1944 to join the Headquarters of the 3rd or Home Counties Division. Ten days later, he was blown up on a Teller mine. The explosion threw him up into a tree, taking off his left leg at the knee and so damaging the right leg that it had to be amputated.

The Shepperds' home was in Upper Gordon Road, Camberley, where Lesley was active in the Red Cross and on liaison duties with the Free French quartered in the town. Lesley only heard of her husband's potentially fatal injuries indirectly. The first indication that something was wrong was the arrival of a note, dictated by Alan to

the nurse in the Casualty Clearing Station, in which he said, 'they had to take off the other'. Two weeks after sustaining his terrible injuries there were still only vague stories. Then Lesley received another dictated letter, from Llandough, Wales, short on detail but telling her he was going to be all right. This time, the letter bore a telephone number. When she rang, the sister said: 'Come quickly, your husband is dying'. A crowded troop train took her to Cardiff where she changed trains for Llandough. On alighting onto the platform, a female porter approached her. 'Are you Mrs Shepperd?', the girl asked. On hearing the affirmative, the porter said her boyfriend had moved Alan Shepperd into hospital. 'These are for you', the girl said, handing over a bunch of flowers. For Lesley, who had quietly harboured her innermost fears that Alan might be brain damaged or blind, this act of kindness left her in tears on that small Welsh platform.

When they were reunited for the first time, she knew he would be all right. He tackled his disability with doggedness and determination, even refusing to read newspapers lest it might distract him from focusing upon his recovery. Lesley knew she had to have Alan

'Individuals reacted differently according to their situation, experience and emotions.'

moved closer to home, but it needed the intervention of a Member of Parliament to do that. Alan was transferred to Roehampton and had the great good fortune to become a patient of Sir George Perkins, formerly the consultant head surgeon to the British Expeditionary Force in the First World War. Just prior to V-E Day, it was planned to operate yet again on Alan's legs. Lesley asked to see the consultant surgeon. 'The shorter the individual, the easier it is to walk on artificial legs', Sir George told her. Alan had been six feet tall. 'I propose to cut him down by three inches', the surgeon told her. She was having none of that, pointing out that there was nothing in her marriage vows about longer or shorter spouses. Ultimately she settled for a husband one and a half inches shorter.

They were at home on V-E Day. Their street filled with happy and cheering people. While Alan had no feelings for the occasion, it had its effect upon his wife. Her feelings were of great hatred for the Germans, but there was no bitterness. She felt proud that her husband had made his contribution to ultimate peace, and relieved that she still had him. She wondered about the effect of his injuries upon

A V-E Day street party, Ophir Road, Portsmouth. (Portsmouth City Records Office)

their two young children, but did not worry about finance. The assumption was that he would get back into the army, and that is what he did. After his new legs had been fitted and he could walk with two sticks, he bullied the War Office into taking him back. Thus the Shepperds had their own family victory over adversity. 'I have a deep faith in the Almighty', said Lesley. 'I am always worrying God about something.'

The principal universities in the land had made their own contribution to victory and had ample cause to celebrate. Cambridge's infusion of brain power into Bletchley Park is well documented, but what is perhaps less well known is the planning of D-Day conducted in Trinity and St John's colleges, 28-31 March 1944. Cambridge's outpouring of joy occurred on V-E Day out on Midsummer Common, where the mayor lit the celebration bonfire.

The influence the war had on Oxford and Cambridge was marked, although cynics asserted that the Oxbridge colleges had suffered more from wartime visitors than from bombs. Oxford's undergraduate population between 1943–44 largely consisted of those who were under eighteen, medically unfit for military service, or officer cadets on short courses. Undergraduates were not allowed to visit public houses unless they had a meal, college gates were closed at 11pm, and females were only allowed into male colleges between the hours of two and seven o'clock – no doubt on the principle that sex-in-the-afternoon was a decadent French habit which would not be emulated by the sons of English gentlemen.

On V-E Day, there was much dancing around Carfax and kissing in the streets and along the Isis. Town and Gown were in harmony as the girls from the town participated in the latter activity more readily than the ladies of Lady Margaret Hall and Somerville. Out in the Meadows, their bonfire burned.

One undergraduate returned to college at one in the morning after taking part in these activities and putting up a notice outside one of the girls' colleges, which dawn revealed as advertising 'US Servicemen – Bed and Breakfast 10/6d' (52½p). He entered the Junior Common Room, having removed the bars which had been carefully loosened that afternoon, and jumped straight into the arms of the Dean, an Anglo-Catholic clergyman with a lisp, who embraced him warmly and greeted him with the words: 'My dear young man, how enterprising of you to enter college in this way. The front doors, however, have been open all night'. The war had truly begun to open Oxford's doors.

When the University assembled for the Michaelmas Term in October 1945, it was to discover a new breed of undergraduate – elderly gentlemen aged 24 or 25 who had commanded companies and even battalions and destroyers. Proctors and Bulldogs had a merry time chasing them, to their utter incredulity, out of Oxford's public houses. When the University returned after the Christmas vacation, it was to find that all the rules about public houses had been quietly withdrawn. However, no change was made about sex-in-the-afternoon. The war had proved to be a partial solvent but V-E Day had had its impact.

Below the tertiary level of education, in the secondary schools, there were different emotions reflecting the age difference. For the young men who were at school during the war, it had been both the best of times and the worst of times. It was the worst of times because those great gods of the Sixth Form and the Prefects' Common Room, to whom the young men looked up in awe, rapidly became, on leaving school, the casualties of the Italian and Normandy Campaigns, and so the young man in his heart knew that a similar fate might soon overtake him. But it was also the best of times – the time for hope and a time for bright visions of the future. For almost everyone in Britain, V-E Day was a double celebration. It represented the end of fear and the beginning of the new and better world.

At Bletchley Park, the naval people invited the teetotal Margaret Bowers into the Wardroom to celebrate the occasion. Against her better judgement, she drank several tots of navy gin and literally passed out on leaving the hut. At 5pm, she joined in a street party as best she could. For Bletchley, V-E Day was not an end but a pause, because there was still work connected with Japan to be done. Later on, she went up to London to watch the big victory celebration parade. As she stood, as but one individual in the midst of a cheering throng, she felt mixed emotions; guilt that she had not bled during the course of the war, and also a touch of sadness that the Official Secrets' Act meant there would not be similar recognition for work which had been so vital, so intensive, and so shattering.

Dancing around a bonfire in East Acton.

The 18th century bells of St Mary the Virgin, Powerstock, had not rung for over five years. They were part of the wartime alarm system. Now, on the evening of 7 May, their glad peals swept out, up and over the green hills and valleys. People came together to plan the morrow. They had little food, but the village people volunteered to take on cooking and food production for the next day's tea party. One villager spoke of the amazing atmosphere that night. On the big day, while the children ran their races up on Parsons Hill, alongside the unlit bonfire, the women of the village laid the long trestle tables in the village hut with sandwiches and scones, decorating tables with streamers and balloons. (Elsewhere in the land, the street party was a more common feature of this celebration.) Time had also been found to decorate the windows and doors. It was purely a village celebration. The evacuees were long gone. Later on, there were skittles in the school playground and there was also the 'best ankle' competition. A sheet had been hung between two poles, with a gap at the bottom for the display of anonymous ankles. The women had to be

encouraged to take part. One such was Jessie Leaf, the garage proprietor's wife, who allowed her ankles to be judged by Dr Dearlove,
the doctor from Beaminster. She remembers how he felt the ankles
and bones displayed under the sheet – 'felt with good intentions', she
was quick to add. She won the competition. In the evening, the bonfire was lit, one dot of light in a necklace of others running westward
down to Lyme Bay and eastward towards Weymouth and beyond.
Douglas Leaf, the garage proprietor, was unable to contribute any
enlightenment as to how Powerstock had spent V-E Day. 'I remember V-J Day better', he said, 'for that was the day Morgan Biles's bull
rampaged through the village'. There was a more ready recollection
of V-J Day throughout the village. The preparation had not been
quite so hurried. V-E Day had been a beneficial rehearsal for what
turned out to be a grander affair. On V-J Day, the licensee of the
Three Horseshoes Inn festooned the building with coloured lights –
something most unusual for the time and, indeed, the place.

V-E Day meant peace and, throughout the land, there was a standard format of street parties, bonfires and jollifications as that peace
was enthusiastically celebrated. After all, it was an event anticipated
way back, as is apparent from the words of a 1943 song:

> I'm going to get lit up when the lights go up in London,
> I'm going to get lit up as I've never been before;
> You will find me on the tiles, you will find me wreathed in
>   smiles;
> I'm going to get lit up so I'll be visible for miles.

The one area where the occasion passed by and was taken for the
pause it seemed to be, was among servicemen who only the day
before had been on active service. Servicemen in and around
London, however, behaved quite differently, as was recalled by the
Member of Parliament, Tom Driberg:

> In the orange glow that streamed down from the Tivoli to the
> pavement of the Strand, a buxom woman in an apron made of
> a Union Jack and a man of respectable middle class appearance
> did an exaggerated Latin dance while an accordion played
> 'South of the Border' . . . As I picked my unobtrusive way along

Coventry Street, a cheerful woman bawled, 'MPs – yer off duty tonight!' I started guiltily; but she was addressing two Redcaps. On the roof above Scott's dignified Oyster House, an airman and a Yank did a fantastic Harold Lloyd act, elaborately sharing a bottle, tossing coins down to the people, who screamed each time they swayed over the parapet.

London deserved her prominent position as the focus of the nation's celebrations; celebrations which were being held in most of the

A Royal Air Force truck laden with revellers.

capital cities throughout the world. What went on in London on 8 May 1945 was also conducted with shades less enthusiasm and extravagance in the cities and towns throughout the land. Thousands who lived out in the provinces and who were so able, converged upon London for the day. There was Miss S M Andrews, Second Mistress at Tonbridge County School for Girls, who travelled up to the city accompanied by friends. When they heard there was to be a church service in St Paul's they made a bee line for the Cathedral, whose wartime images so represented the spirit and determination which had made victory possible.

The bells had begun pealing at 11.30 and we could hear the choir practising in the distance. There was no pageantry (that will come on Sunday) but a real sense of reverence. After the service, we walked along Fleet Street and the Strand to St James' Park to eat our lunch on the grass in the company of hundreds of others. Everyone was very quiet, just relaxing and bells were ringing all the time. Then we strolled to Parliament Square, past an elderly lady, most respectably dressed, calmly eating her paper bag lunch sitting on the kerb. We stationed ourselves opposite the entrance gates to Parliament Yard, but lost our places when the mob made a sudden dash forward to cheer a car they thought was Churchill's, but the hand making the V sign turned out to be a laughing US soldier's, and we all roared. Thenceforward, mounted police had to clear a separate way for each car and we shoved and pushed and laughed.

At 3 o'clock a loudspeaker broadcast Churchill's declaration: *'Yesterday at 2.41am the representative of the German High Command and government, General Jodl, signed the act of unconditional surrender of all German land, sea and air forces, in Europe, to the Allied Expeditionary Force and to the Soviet High Command. Today, this agreement will be ratified and confirmed at Berlin. Hostilities will end officially at one minute after midnight tonight, Tuesday, 8 May, but in the interest of saving lives the ceasefire began yesterday to be sounded along the fronts. The German war is therefore at an end. Our gratitude to all our splendid allies goes forth from all our hearts in this island and the British Empire. We may allow ourselves a brief period of rejoicing but let us not forget for a moment*

Winston Churchill's broadcast announcing the end of the war.

the toils and efforts that lie ahead. Japan, with all her treachery and greed, remains unsubdued. The injustice she has inflicted upon Great Britain and the United States, and other countries, and her detestable cruelties call for justice and retribution. We must now devote all our strength and resources to the completion of our task both at home and abroad. Advance Britannia! Long live the cause of freedom! God save the King!'

. . . and there was some cheering but a sense of disappointment until Churchill's car was spotted coming from Downing Street to the Commons.

The Commons was waiting, yet it took Churchill's car 30 minutes to travel the quarter of a mile. The car was mobbed by those wishing to thank him, shouting 'Good Old Winnie'. Some who were there described how moved the great man looked, even shedding a tear. At one stage, he stood on the front seat of the open car, acknowledging the crowds. 'Thank you all, thank you very much.' 'We were within a few yards and could see him clearly', continued Miss Andrews,

Winston Churchill, his car hidden from view, giving his famous V for Victory sign.

He looked very youthful but sober and had his cigar and the V sign as he sat on the hood. We all let off steam there and no mistake. Then along to Buckingham Palace where again were thousands hoping to see the Royal Family. Everyone shouted 'We want the King' and when no sign of life appeared, someone shouted 'Is anyone at home?', and another, 'We want George!' Just as we were considering fading away, suddenly they appeared on the balcony, the Queen and Princess Margaret in electric blue, the King in naval uniform, and Princess Elizabeth in ATS (Auxiliary Territorial Service) uniform. Again we yelled, and satisfied, walked back to Charing Cross.

Gunner William Mitchell and two dozen servicemen travelled up to London on a lorry coming from East Anglia. Mitchell was a member of Anti-Aircraft Command stationed at Woodbridge, north-east of Ipswich. He knew that hostilities would end on 8 May, and that some sort of public celebration would be taking place on an historic occasion. I do not think anyone bothered with leave passes on that day. I just told my officer that I would like the day off and hitch-hiked to London.

As they passed through Ipswich, the church bells were ringing. Masses of flags were out, as were the townspeople, dressed up in their best clothes, with no apparent destination. In the centre of the town

The King, the Queen and the two princesses on the balcony of Buckingham Palace acknowledging the V-E Day crowd.

stood a great throng of people, and others, strolling nonchalantly around as though on a Bank Holiday. It was a fine, sunny day, yet most people carried coats or macs. A couple of boys who passed the truck rode bicycles decorated as though they were entering a May Day procession. On the way towards London, the truck's passengers observed an array of flags and bunting, some obviously relics from the Jubilee and Coronation. People in the streets waved as they headed home to be with their families or to join in the general festivities. At Chelmsford the threatening rain made its appearance, but by the time they reached Warley the sun again shone through. At Ilford it was noticeable how the queues at bus stops were growing with people heading into the city. The truck stopped at the traffic lights beside a pub. The customers gave out a cheer for those aboard and a plump young clippie paused in her quaffing of a pint of ale, shouting to the men in her Cockney voice, "I bet you'd like a drink of this 'ere". The lights changed to green and they were off.

Disembarking at Manor House, the potential revellers found long queues at the bus stops, but the underground was strangely quiet. The city centre-bound train was full of folk all dressed up and looking as though they were expecting something exciting to happen. Along the way, a group of Canadians got in and chattered in the loud tones of North Americans, of their hopes for an extension of leave. Before the doors had closed completely, three young men wearing carnival hats eased them apart and entered the carriage carrying bundles of flags on long sticks. The train virtually emptied itself at Piccadilly. Outside, in the Circus, a large crowd stood basking in the bright sunshine with an ubiquitous air of expectancy. Two Canadian soldiers stood on, or rather were hanging on to, the top of the concrete covering to the Eros statue plinth. There were bangs in the crowds as people let off fireworks. A sea of people flowed down Lower Regent Street, gravitating towards the Mall and Trafalgar Square. Most of them carried some kind of flag – understandably, Union Jacks were predominant – and there was a sprinkling of rattles and carnival hats. One ATS girl had managed to fix a Union Jack with a two feet long stick pushed through her hat band. She moved towards Trafalgar Square with the Union Jack flying from her hat as though on the prow of a battleship. In the Square itself, there was not an inch of spare room as people covered the roadway, pavements, fountains and the base of Nelson's

Column. Up in Shaftesbury Avenue, a Soviet officer was being carried on shoulders whilst everyone rushed to shake hands with him, pat him on the back, or even just to touch him. He sat there, smiling, hugely embarrassed.

In the Canadian Beaver Club overlooking the Square, the lounge began to fill as people took their seats before the Prime Minister's broadcast. The windows were open and, as Mr Churchill spoke, those inside could see the flow of people moving into Trafalgar Square and down towards Buckingham Palace. All the while, the club members listened to the broadcast without a sound or comment. Then, at the end of Mr Churchill's speech, buglers sounded 'Cease Fire' and, as the last notes faded, it was followed by his words, 'God Save the King'. Those who had been sitting there that afternoon stood for the National Anthem and then quickly filed out of the room.

As those who had been inside the Club stood surveying the scene across the Square, the crowd seemed even larger and more dense. Down Charing Cross Road came a crawling stream of vehicles, all

'Every vehicle had a covering of humans.' A truck passing through the Strand, London.

covered with a mass of people on the roofs and hanging on to running boards and anything they could cling on to. Two Australians were standing on the top of a tram, trying to make progress up the Strand. A surge of people pushed under Admiralty Arch towards the Mall. The crowd in Northumberland Avenue and along the Embankment was thinner, but Westminster Bridge and Parliament Square were jam-packed. A line of Reconnaissance Regiment soldiers came along, singing their song: 'Far away – far away – oh she pushed for a Recce who was far, far aw-a-ay!' They bumped into a line of Land Army Girls going in the opposite direction. In Parliament Square, two RAF men stood on the cross arms of a tall lamp standard, a truck full of ex-prisoners of war received a tremendous cheer, and an ambulance driven by a hefty woman driver with a grin all over her face made a nasty casualty of someone's bicycle. Every vehicle had a covering of humans, all singing away.

When the Prime Minister made his belated appearance in the House of Commons, Members from both sides of the House rose and cheered, waving their order papers. People in the normally sedate Galleries also got to their feet and cheered. Some in the House were overcome by the emotion of the event. For his part, Churchill smiled, appearing shy, even embarrassed before moving 'That this House do now attend at the Church of St Margaret, Westminster, to give humble and reverent thanks to Almighty God for our deliverance from the threat of German dominance'. Led out by the Sergeant-at-Arms, the Commons repaired itself to church to give thanks and to remember the 21 Members who had given their lives in the war.

After church, the Prime Minister took his leave for Buckingham Palace via Downing Street (to pick up a fresh supply of cigars). After an appearance on the balcony with the Royal Family, he drove to the Ministry of Health building, where he was scheduled to make his second broadcast of the day. The balcony where he was due to appear was wreathed in bunting. Several newsreel cars, mostly American and Canadian, stood in front of the building. There were cameras set up in the windows opposite, to take photographs of the event. By 5pm, the scheduled time of Churchill's appearance, the crowd had become very dense indeed. Several women fainted. Cameramen made the most of their extra time by making final adjustments to their

Winston Churchill with King George VI on the balcony of Buckingham Palace.

equipment, while an American broadcaster tinkered with his script. 'After 5pm the crowd began to get impatient', recalls Mitchell.

> Sundry officials who appeared at the balcony for a moment were given a rousing cheer; two girls on the Ministry building getting out on to the balcony and showing a nifty pair of legs got the usual whistle used in such circumstances and some wise-cracks.

A section of the crowd began to clap in rhythm. 'Why are we waiting' was sung to the tune of 'O come all ye faithful'. Then there was 'One, two, three, four, what the hell are we waiting for?', followed by 'We Want Winnie'. Two cameramen unintentionally teased the crowd by peering into the interior of the building and adjusting their cameras, only to calm the masses by settling back into their original positions. People on the rooftops opposite kept those below amused by sending paper aeroplanes in the air, while the crowd followed their descent with impatient eyes. Two drunken sailors appeared at the door of the Ministry building, to a huge cheer – that was the mood of the crowd; prepared to cheer anyone or anything.

Just before 6pm Churchill, accompanied by Ernest Bevin, Herbert Morrison and other Cabinet members, appeared on the balcony. Once the enthusiastic cheering had died down, he began the delivery of his speech:

> This is your victory. It is the victory of the cause of freedom in every land. In all our long history we have never seen a greater day than this. Everyone, man or woman, has done his best. Everyone has tried. Neither the long years, nor the dangers, nor the fierce attacks of the enemy, have in any way weakened the deep resolve of the British nation. God bless you all.

Winston Churchill waving from the balcony of the Ministry of Health building acknowledges the crowd. 'This is your victory' he tells them.

The people cheered until they were hoarse, and when they had finished they shuffled away like great armies of tightly packed sardines.

Piccadilly at 7pm was in a state of turmoil. Circles of people danced and sang. A north London piece entitled 'Knees up Muvver Brahn' was by far the most popular. On the balcony of the American

Red Cross Rainbow Corner, the USAAF band played to a crowd which had choked the entrance into Shaftesbury Avenue. A wave of people moving up from the Circus met the immovable force of those endeavouring to come down. The former were carried away in a pushing match won by the latter. The singing continued unabated. All the old songs were trotted out: 'Tipperary', 'Pack up your Troubles' and 'Shine on, shine on Harvest Moon'.

Quite naturally, the pubs between Shaftesbury Avenue and Oxford Street had not escaped the revellers' attention. They were full to overflowing. Customers were taking their glasses and drinking in the streets – a habit not unusual in Paris, but unknown in London. Where there was the case of two pubs opposite one another, it was impossible to tell who was drinking in which pub. Glasses were in short supply and consequently the committed drinkers were carrying their own captured glass from pub to pub. At about 8pm, the first peacetime disaster to hit the city was beginning to reveal itself. First one pub, then another and another, ran out of beer. A great trek then began to find the places which still had stocks of beer. For those without the inclination, the capacity or the cash, there remained the attraction of dancing in the street. Outside one pub, two Cockney

Happy crowds of soldiers, sailors, airmen and civilians in front of the American Rainbow Red Cross Corner after the announcement of the surrender, 7 May 1945.

ladies kept the crowd amused with their own, classical interpretation of that oft-repeated dance peculiar to London, 'Muvver Brahn'. Close by, some Americans jitterbugged with ATS girls. A circle of French sailors engaged in their own tongue one of their own, female, nationals, who was among a number of women working that night. Other highly painted women of the same calling promenaded themselves shamelessly in front of men who by now, if they had had any intentions, had long since lost the capability. Surprisingly that night, there were very few, overt displays of drunkenness.

At twilight on V-E Day, Mitchell was back in Piccadilly amidst swirling rings of happy people singing, dancing, laughing and kissing. Half way up the side of the London Pavilion he spotted a lone air cadet sitting, perched on the metalwork of the lifeless neon signs and advertisements. The boy was singing away and waving, as though he had no cares in the world. From out of the windows of the Criterion shone the beams of two searchlights, bathing everyone in a brilliance of light Piccadilly had not seen for years. The black-out had given way to a dim out in September 1944 but, on V-E night, searchlights sought out one another to form Vs in the sky. Under one tall lamp standard, a captain was running a competition to stick a paper hat atop the lamp.

A Canadian tried, a sailor, an Aussie, a young ATC, they all got to the last few feet, struggled as the crowd roared its encouragement, and then slipped down, with battered trousers and torn hands. Around the base of Eros sat a ring of civvies and policemen, the latter just taking the night off, smoking and enjoying themselves in the place that had kept them busy at nights for so long.

In Coventry Street, an American in the RAF held a woman in a passionate embrace. His clothes were in shreds, his shoulders so ripped that his sleeves hung on by only a few threads. Half a dozen people were enjoying themselves, dancing, singing and jumping on a metal door which lay in the road. A cornet player in Leicester Square had attracted a group of singers around him. Close by, an enterprising small band with a trumpet, accordion and saxophone played jazz for energetic jitterbugs. Outside a cinema, a man took a collection among a crowd watching a woman give a hula-hula exhibition. Outside another cinema in the Square, a crowd gathered to watch workmen finishing a V-E Day tableau by the hauling up of a massive painting of Stalin to join those of Churchill and Truman. Since the Soviet Union became an ally in 1941, posters of a smiling Stalin, the Uncle Joe of popular usage, had decorated many hoardings and had contained, of course, no reference to the purges and the Gulag.

Seated on the steps of Saint Martin's was a throng of middle-aged people and children being conducted in community singing. In Trafalgar Square, people watched Verey lights fired from the National Gallery, and enjoyed the challenge of avoiding them when they came to ground. Uniquely, Admiralty Arch, the National Gallery and Saint Martin's were bathed for the first time in years in floodlighting. Two searchlights on Admiralty Arch chose to light Nelson at random atop his column, while down Whitehall, Big Ben stood out in its own floodlighting.

It was a pleasant, warm evening. Many of the men were in shirt-sleeves, and girls in summer dresses gave an impression of people on a seaside Bank Holiday – that is, with the exception of the noise that evening. The Palace could be seen down the Mall 'in a slightly orange light'. The suspensions of passing cars were severely tested as the crowd grasped out and hung on to anything they could find. The flow of people which had caused difficulties to cyclists trying to push their cycles in an opposite direction, frustrated for a long while the efforts of an RAF officer in his smart sports car, to move beyond the Victoria monument. He suffered a severe sense of humour failure when, uninvited, people clambered over his prized possession. Mitchell observed how

> it drove away nevertheless with two standing on the rear luggage rack which gave way, depositing its luggage in the road and rattled on behind the rest of the car like something coming away from a wedding.

Across in St James' Park a bonfire roared, sending sparks up into the sky. Perched on top of Victoria Monument was a battery of cameras. Below them stood a crowd, cheering and shouting: 'We want the King', 'Two, four, six, eight, who do we appreciate – George!' and

'The Palace could be seen down the Mall in a slightly orange light.'

the song 'Come out, come out wherever you are'. Mitchell was among that crowd, taking everything in.

A light switched on for a few minutes in the Palace behind the balcony, renewing the cheers of expectation. A nondescript band marched its way into the crowd, playing the French national anthem. On the statue on the Monument, a RAF man was sitting on the statue's shoulders, silhouetted against the floodlighting and waving a flag. Someone climbed the gate of the Palace and energetically led·the crowd in singing until he was removed by the police. A guard picquet being marched past the front wall of the Palace itself got a rousing reception. The light came on again behind the balcony, and cheering broke out again and rose to a huge roar as Their Majesties appeared for this, the eighth and final time. They stood for five minutes as the crown roared its welcome. The King waved several times and the crowd burst into renewed efforts at cheering. Finally, as Their Majesties left the balcony, was heard 'For He's a Jolly

Good Fellow' and the National Anthem. Although it was now well past eleven o'clock, the two young princesses, escorted by army officers, slipped out of the palace and into the crowd to savour the atmosphere.

Up at Trafalgar Square, at half past midnight, the crowd was thinning, but in Piccadilly it was as dense as it had been at 1pm. A huge roar of protest went up as the searchlights were turned off. Along Regent Street, the drift homeward had begun. There were bodies in doorways and on the pavements, of people with no means of returning whence they had come, so they had settled down for the night. Close to Oxford Circus, a bonfire blazed in the middle of the street while a local in a top hat waved a large Union Jack and led the onlookers in singing and dancing. When a fire engine arrived to put out the fire, it was greeted with hoots and boos from the crowd. The scene was much the same along Oxford Street and Edgware Road, where the people were flowing out of town. A solitary man stood in a doorway holding a tray of V-badges for sale. He said not a word, and no one stopped to buy.

There were, of course, in London on V-E Day the wives of husbands still away. Their emotions were mixed; happy that their loved ones had survived, yet sad that they could not be with them to celebrate victory. This extract from a letter to a Commander Royal Navy from his wife, written on 9 May, is a good example of the feelings of one of the wives-in-waiting:

My darling,

I thought of you so much yesterday, watching the "VE-Day" crowds from my office window, and wondered where you were and if you were able to celebrate peace-in-Europe and longed so much for you to be home here with me. The crowds in Whitehall were an amazing sight from my office, we had a grand-stand view of everything that went on. It was one of those hot stuffy days and people were fainting in all directions. Everybody was very good tempered though and even by the evening, there were surprisingly few drunks about . . .

I met one of my second officers in Piccadilly and we both felt pretty exhausted and very thirsty and hot, so made our way to the Berkeley Buttery and had a couple of gin and tonics to celebrate V-E Day. I drank your health sweetheart and wished so much we could have been together for it.

I then walked all the way back to Chelsea as no buses were running and got back in a state of complete exhaustion with my feet many sizes too big for my shoes! It was wonderful to see all the sky lit up with floodlights at night, even the Battersea Power Station across the river looked really lovely.

A different view, to be found in Jonathan Croall's *Don't You Know There's a War On? – The People's Voice 1939–1945*, or certainly one from a different angle, was provided by an art student who, accompanied by her fellow student boyfriend, had gone into town. Her feelings at the time were ones of relief; relief that she wouldn't 'live each day in dread and fear'. Whenever those in her art group made rendezvous in town, it was invariably at the 'Nat Gal' – the National Gallery – a rather reasonable meeting place for students of art. She and her boyfriend watched the goings on from the top of the steps:

Soldiers and girls dancing in a street near Berkeley Square.

There were crowds of people charging about, surging, shouting and dancing in their own little circles. A vast, snake-like procession was coming down Charing Cross Road, young girls and American soldiers, and amongst them, carried shoulder high, a naked man crowned with silver leaves waving a chamber pot. It was all very happy, very noisy and no violence.

The two students, whose relationship had not progressed beyond the kissing stage, sat holding hands on a grassy patch below the parapet. They discussed arty matters of light and shade whilst next to them

was a couple, copulating. I was fascinated that for the occasion they had both taken off their shoes, and *only* their shoes, and placed them neatly side by side on the grass, just as though they were in a hotel, and had put their shoes out for cleaning. Copulation was certainly the order of the day – or night . . .

After midnight, they walked home via Euston, Camden Town and Hampstead. Despite the lateness of the hour there were still parties going on in the side streets.

The houses and streets were hung with bunting, and tables and chairs were out in the road, large fat mums were kicking up their heels, while dirty children were dropping off to sleep amongst the remains of celebratory meals.

One very interesting, detached view of what happened in London on V-E Day was provided by Mollie Panter-Downes, London correspondent of the *New Yorker*, and is taken from *London War Notes 1939–1945*. She sent regular reports from London to America throughout the course of the war in Europe.

The big day started off here with a coincidence. In the last hours of peace, in September, 1939, a violent thunderstorm broke over the city, making a lot of people think for a moment that the first air raid had begun. Early Tuesday morning, V-E Day, nature tidily brought the war to an end with an imitation of a blitz so realistic that many Londoners started awake and

A large bonfire in Havering Street, Stepney, on V-E night, one of many lighting up the sky over London.

reached blurrily for the bedside torch. Then they remembered, and, sighing with relief, fell asleep again as the thunder rolled over the capital, already waiting with its flags. The decorations had blossomed on the streets Monday afternoon. By six that night, Piccadilly Circus and all the city's other focal points were jammed with a cheerful, expectant crowd waiting for an official statement from Downing Street. Movie cameramen crouched patiently on the rooftops. When a brewer's van rattled by and the driver leaned out and yelled 'It's all over', the crowd cheered, then went on waiting. Presently, word spread that the announcement would be delayed, and the day, which had started off like a rocket, began to fizzle slowly and damply out.

When the day finally came, it was like no other day that anyone can remember. It had a flavour of its own, an extemporaneousness which gave it something of the quality of a vast, happy village fête as people wandered about, sat, sang, and slept against a summer background of trees, grass, flowers, and water. It was not, people said, like the 1918 Armistice Day, for at no time was the reaction hysterical. It was not like the Coronation, for the crowds were larger and their gaiety, which held up all through the night, was obviously not picked up in a pub. The day also surprised the prophets who had said that only the young would be resilient enough to celebrate in a big way. Apparently, the desire to assist in London's celebration combusted spontaneously in the bosom of every member of every family, from the smallest babies, with their hair done up in red-white-and-blue ribbons, to beaming elderly couples who, utterly without self-consciousness, strolled up and down the streets arm in arm in red-white-and-blue paper hats. Even the dogs wore immense tricoloured bows. Rosettes sprouted from the slabs of pork in the butcher shops, which, like other food stores, were open for a couple of hours in the morning. With their customary practicality, housewives put bread before circuses. They waited in the long bakery queues, the string bags of the common round in one hand and the Union Jack of the glad occasion in the other. Even queues seemed tolerable that morning. The bells had begun to peal and, after the storm, London was having that perfect, hot, English summer's day which, one sometimes feels, is to be found only in the imaginations of the lyric poets.

The girls in their thin, bright dresses heightened the impression that the city had been taken over by an enormous family picnic. The number of extraordinarily pretty young girls, who presumably are hidden on working days inside the factories and government offices, was astonishing. They streamed out into the parks and streets like flocks of twittering, gaily plumaged cockney birds. In their freshly curled hair were cornflowers and poppies, and they wore red-white-and-blue ribbons around their narrow waists. Some of them even tied ribbons around their bare ankles. Strolling with their uniformed boys, arms candidly about each other, they provided a constant, gay, simple marginal decoration to the big, solemn moments of the day. The crowds milled back and forth between the Palace, Westminster, Trafalgar Square, and Piccadilly Circus, and when they got tired they simply sat down wherever they happened to be – on the grass, on doorsteps, or on the curb – and watched the other people or spread handkerchiefs over their faces and

Two British sailors wading in the Trafalgar Square fountains with two of the many pretty girls who emerged to celebrate V-E Day.

took a nap. Everybody appeared determined to see the King and Queen and Mr Churchill at least once, and few could have been disappointed. One small boy, holding onto his father's hand, wanted to see the trench shelters in Green Park too. 'You don't want to see shelters today', his father said. 'You'll never have to use them again, son.' 'Never?' the child asked doubtfully. 'Never!' the man cried, almost angrily. *'Never!* Understand?' In the open space before the Palace, one of the places where the Prime Minister's speech was to be relayed by loudspeaker at three o'clock, the crowds seemed a little intimidated by the nearness of that symbolic block of gray stone. The people who chose to open their lunch baskets and munch sandwiches there among the flowerbeds of tulips were rather subdued. Piccadilly Circus attracted the more demonstrative spirits.

By lunchtime, in the Circus, the buses had to slow to a crawl in order to get through the tightly packed, laughing people. A lad in the black beret of the Tank Corps was the first to climb the little pyramidal Angkor Wat of scaffolding and sandbags which was erected early in the war to protect the pedestal of the Eros statue after the figure had been removed to safekeeping. The boy shinned up to the top and took a tiptoe Eros pose, aiming an imaginary bow, while the crowd roared. He was followed by a paratrooper in a maroon beret, who, after getting up to the top, reached down and hauled up a blond young women in a very tight pair of green slacks. When she got to the top, the Tank Corps soldier promptly grabbed her in his arms and, encouraged by ecstatic cheers from the whole Circus, seemed about to enact the classic rôle of Eros right on the top of the monument. Nothing came of it, because a moment later a couple of GIs joined them and before long the pyramid was covered with boys and girls. They sat jammed together in an affectionate mass, swinging their legs over the sides, wearing

Showers of paper cascading from the windows of a building in Davies Street, onto soldiers and civilians below provided a gentle form of celebration.

The concrete covering of the Eros statue plinth, Piccadilly Circus, proved to be no obstacle to determined celebrators.

each other's uniform caps, and calling down wisecracks to the crowd. 'My God', someone said, 'think of a flying bomb coming down on this!' When a firecracker went off, a hawker with a tray of tin brooches of Monty's head happily yelled that comforting, sometimes fallacious phrase of the Blitz nights, 'All right, mates, it's one of ours!'

All day long, the deadly past was for most people only just under the surface of the beautiful, safe present – so much so that the government decided against sounding the sirens in a triumphant 'all clear' for fear that the noise would revive too many painful memories. For the same reason, there were no salutes of guns – only the pealing of the bells and the whistles of tugs on the Thames sounding the doot, doot, doot, dooooot of the V, and the roar of the planes, which swooped back and forth over the city, dropping red and green signals toward the blur of smiling, upturned faces.

It was without any doubt Churchill's day. Thousands of King George's subjects wedged themselves in front of the Palace throughout the day, chanting ceaselessly 'We want the King' and

'Each group danced its own dance, sang its own song, and went its own way as the spirit moved it.'

cheering themselves hoarse when he and the Queen and their daughters appeared, but when the crowd saw Churchill, there was a deep, full-throated, almost reverent roar. He was at the head of a procession of Members of Parliament, walking back to the House of Commons from the traditional St Margaret's Thanksgiving Service. Instantly, he was surrounded by people – people running, standing on tiptoe, holding up babies so that they could be told later they had seen him, and shouting affectionately the absurd little nurserymaid name, 'Winnie, Winnie!' One of two happily sozzled, very old, and incredibly dirty cockneys who had been engaged in a slow, shuffling dance, like a couple of Shakespearean clowns, bellowed, 'That's 'im, that's 'is little old lovely bald 'ead!' The crowds saw Churchill again later, when he emerged from the Commons and was driven off in the back of a small open car, rosy, smiling, and looking immensely happy. Ernest Bevin, following in another car, got a cheer, too. Herbert Morrison, sitting unobtrusively in a corner of a third car, was hardly recognised, and the other Cabinet Ministers did no better. The crowd had ears, eyes and throats for no one but Churchill, and for him everyone in it seemed to have the hearing, sight, and lungs of fifty men. His slightly formal official broadcast, which was followed by buglers sounding the 'cease firing' call, did not strike the emotional note that had been expected, but he hit it perfectly in his subsequent informal speech ('My dear friends, this is your victory . . .') from a Whitehall balcony.

All day long, little extra celebrations started up. In the Mall, a model of a Gallic cock waltzed on a pole over the heads of the singing people. 'It's the Free French', said someone. The Belgians in the crowd tagged along after a Belgian flag that marched by, its bearer invisible. A procession of students raced through Green Park, among exploding squibs, clashing dustbin lids like cymbals and waving an immense Jeyes Disinfectant poster as a banner. American sailors and laughing girls formed a conga line down the middle of Piccadilly, and cockneys linked arms in the Lambeth Walk. It was a day and night of no fixed plan and no organised merriment. Each group danced its own dance, sang its own song, and went its own way as the spirit moved it. The most tolerant, self-effacing people in London on V-E Day were the police, who simply stood by, smiling benignly, while soldiers swung by one arm from lamp standards and laughing groups tore down hoardings to build the evening's bonfires. Actually, the police were not unduly strained. The extraordinary thing about the crowds was that they were almost all sober. The number of drunks one saw in that whole day and night could have been counted on two hands – possibly because the pubs were sold out so early. The young service men and women who swung arm in arm down the middle of every street, singing and swarming over the few cars rash enough to come out, were simply happy with an immense holiday happiness. Just before the King's speech, at nine Tuesday night, the big lamps outside the Palace came on and there were cheers and ohs from children who had never seen anything of that kind in their short, blacked-out lives.

The King said:

Today we give thanks to God for a great deliverance. Speaking from our Empire's oldest capital city, war battered, but never for one moment daunted or dismayed, speaking from London, I ask you to join with me in that act of thanksgiving . . . Let us remember those who will not come back . . . the men and women in all the Services who have laid down their lives . . . Then let us salute in proud gratitude the great host of the living who have brought us to victory . . . Armed or unarmed, men and women, you have fought, striven and endured to your utmost. No one knows that better than I do; and I as your King thank you with a full heart . . . With these memories in our minds, let us think what it was that has upheld us through nearly six years of suffering and peril; the knowledge that everything was at stake, our freedom, our independence, our very existence as people . . . We knew that if we failed the last remaining barrier against a world-wide tyranny would have fallen. But we did not fail. Let us . . . on this day of just triumph and proud sorrow . . . take up our work again, resolved as a people to do nothing unworthy of those who died for us and to make the world such a world as they would have desired, for their children and for ours.

As the evening wore on, most of the public buildings were floodlighted. The night was as warm as midsummer, and London, its shabbiness now hidden and its domes and remaining Wren spires warmed by lights and bonfires, was suddenly magnificent. The handsomest building of all was the National Gallery, standing out honey-coloured near a ghostly, blue-shadowed St Martin's and the Charles I bit of Whitehall. The floodlighted face of Big Ben loomed like a kind moon.

So it was in London on V-E Day. The war in Europe was over, a great evil had been defeated. In the words of the King, not, be it noted, in those of a left-wing visionary, or the Army Bureau of Current Affairs pamphlets (explained later in this book), the people were resolved 'to do nothing unworthy of those who died for [us] and to make the world such a world as they would have desired, for their children and for ours'. The celebration was both about victory and about what so many hoped would follow – a better world.

'The floodlighted face of Big Ben loomed like a kind moon.'

But as much as people may have wished, the reality of a continuing war in the Far East could not be easily set aside. 'We must not forget', said Churchill, 'that beyond lurks Japan, harrassed and failing, but still a people of a hundred millions, for whose warriors death has few terrors'. The 14th Army was still engaged with the Japanese in Burma. Peace in Europe meant, therefore, that the 'Forgotten Army' might now be afforded the resources it had thus far been denied. The Servicemen who had secured victory in Europe now faced up to the prospect of redeploying to face the threat in the East. Also in the east there were, of course, 80,000 British prisoners of war in the uncaring hands of the Japanese.

After the British prisoners had been repatriated from German and Italian prison camps, it was discovered that two per cent had died in custody. But over one quarter of Japan's prisoners of war died in their camps and, for many of the rehabilitated, there was the prospect of a much reduced life. In those camps which had clandestine radios, the news of V-E Day encouraged the great multitude that had endured over three years of dreadful treatment to hang on. Where there were no radios there was the rumour mill, and what a double-edged weapon that proved to be.

Twenty-one-year-old W 'Billy' Griffiths was among a number of RAF men to escape to Java before the fall of Singapore. It proved to be a case of 'out of the frying pan, into the fire' when the Dutch authorities in Java capitulated. A few days after being captured by the Japanese, the RAF men were taken up country and forced to disarm booby traps. No sooner had Billy Griffiths got down to do this at the point of a rifle and bayonet than 'the whole lot went off'. He lost his eyes, his hands, and had his leg badly broken. As luck would have it, a passing convoy dropped him off at the Allied Emergency Hospital situated in a converted school. The surgeon there was an Australian, Colonel Edward Dunlop (later Sir Edward). Equally fortunate was Griffiths' youth and fitness as well as a reasonable availability of medical supplies this early in the war.

Billy Griffiths was shown no favours. In three and a half years of imprisonment he was kept in six different camps – an unpleasant experience for anyone. On one occasion, he was beaten across the face for not bowing to a Japanese guard, but for the most part he was looked after by fellow prisoners. The Japanese were not signatories

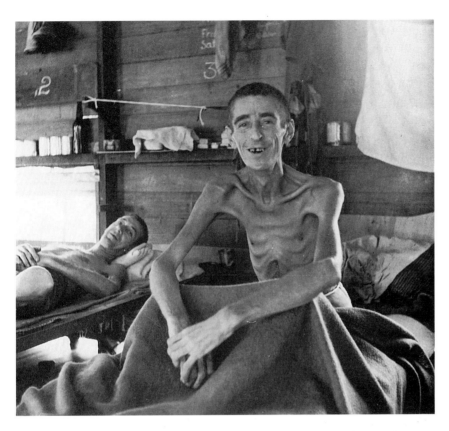

A British Prisoner of War,
Changi Jail, Singapore.

to the Geneva Conventions, refusing to distribute the Red Cross parcels which might have prevented some of the men starving to death. They heard rumours that the European war was going well, but there was no definite news. They were reluctant to give rumours too much credence. 'Some rumours devastated us. Morale would soar in expectation, only to be cruelly dashed when truth dawned, leaving us totally demoralised.' Then one or two Americans who had been shot down arrived in their camp. They updated the prisoners with the news, and a week before 15 August there was definite news that the war in the Pacific was proceeding well. Then there was news of the 'big bomb' attacks on Japan. They were not called atom bombs then. So, V-J Day just came and it was all over with.

I arrived home in Blackpool in mid-November via Singapore and Bombay to Liverpool. I remember my homecoming. There was thick fog and the dockers were on strike. Looking back, I have sad feelings. In wartime, you expect to risk being shot or bombed, but not to die of starvation. I would not dash out to buy a Japanese car.

A study of even the darkest period of the war reveals that usually, not far below the surface, there lay a rich seam of infectious British humour. One tale at war's end which fits ideally within the chronology of this book concerns R C Huntriss. He had spent three and a half years as a Japanese prisoner of war, mostly in Siam on the 'Death Railway'. He returned to England in October 1945, landing in Liverpool where he underwent a brief medical examination before going home. All things considered he was in reasonable shape but, after so long a period on a diet consisting largely of boiled rice and fresh air, he was understandably underweight. It was decided that he needed extra eggs and milk to build him up again. Both these commodities were still rationed and, in order that he could obtain the

The 'big bomb' dropped over Hiroshima at 0815, 6 August 1945 by the B-29 Superfortress Enola Gay was modestly known as 'Little Boy'. Almost 80,000 civilians died.

additional supplies he was deemed to need, he was handed a chit, signed by an army medical officer. It read: 'I certify that you are an expectant mother, date of confinement unknown'. This was the only avenue through which the extra eggs and milk could be released.

In due course, dressed in the uniform of a Lieutenant, Royal Artillery, he presented himself at the local Food Office. He announced that he was an expectant mother and produced his chit by way of proof. The lady behind the table seemed a little surprised but entirely unruffled. 'How awkward for you', she said, handing the pregnant subaltern a further piece of paper for production to retailers of eggs and milk. 'I am not much of a milk drinker, and no extra eggs were available' recounted Mr Huntriss in 1995. 'It remains only to add that I am still "expecting", but hope is fading.'

Finally, as Edward Murch, the former coder on HMS *Prince of Wales* wrote:

> Sad to say
> I cannot recall what I did
> On VE-Day.
> I must have rejoiced with everyone else, of course,
> That the war in Europe was won
> So we could turn all our strength to the East
> Against the Land of the Rising Sun.
>
> And that's another sad thing:
> I cannot remember what I did
> On V-J Day either.
> But I'm sure I was glad
> *The Prince* and *Repulse* were avenged;
> And the slit-eyed evils that went on behind barbed wire
> Were somewhat revenged.
>
> Not long after
> I turned myself back into a civilian,
> Looked around for a wife,
> And tried to get on with the rest of my life.

POSTSCRIPT

Three Peers, the War and Peace

Today, it is difficult to imagine the importance of radio in keeping the public informed and entertained throughout the dark war years and into the period when, at last, a glimmer appeared at the end of the tunnel of general war. The postscript of this book begins with comments made by the Yorkshire author J B Priestley. Within the BBC's weekly repertoire, there were definite highlights: the World News, Tommy Handley's ITMA (It's That Man Again), Woman's Hour, Workers' Playtime and Children's Hour among others. Among the 'others' was a slot on Sunday after the Nine O'clock News, called Postscript, and one of the popular presenters was J B Priestley because he fostered in his devoted listeners' minds their dreams of an egalitarian England and the hope that their lot would improve at the war's end. His broadcast of 17 May 1945 had particular significance. It seemed to signify the wrapping up of over five years of war and the opening of the way for the setting loose of the new social and political forces which had had to be bottled up if the war was to be successfully prosecuted.

> We lived at last in a community with a noble common purpose, and the experience was not only novel but exhilarating. We had a glimpse then of what life might be if men and women freely dedicated themselves, not to their appetites and prejudices, their vanities and fears, but to some great common task . . . We were, you see, better people than we had thought.

Great Britain had begun the war as two nations – the working classes and the middle and upper classes. The war drew both sides together to reflect upon what they had, what they did not have, and what they ought to have; in that respect it had been the crucible of the contemporary world. The catalyst for change was the relative freedom of information. It was a two-way process. Each military theatre of operations had its own newspaper and there were correspondence columns which positively encouraged soldiers to complain. North Africa's *Union Jack* was edited by Captain Hugh Cudlip, the future 'publish and be damned' editor of the *Daily Mirror*. What had prevented an earlier interchange of information had been the attitude and domination of the generals. Kitchener had been regarded with almost God-like reverence, and Haig with such enormous respect that the military arm had been barely subordinate to its supposed political masters. In 1939, the generals tried to begin where they left off in 1918 and, under Chamberlain, did seem to be having their way – they were directly involved in the sacking of the progressive minister, Hore-Belisha. Then Churchill came on the scene, prepared to sack any general who did not come up to the mark and, in that manner, re-adjusted the political/military relationship. Throughout the military's entire order of battle, departments sprang up which had previously not been deemed as necessary. In the Second World War, Public Relations came of age.

A new, almost revolutionary initiative had been the forming of the Army Bureau of Current Affairs (ABCA). The conduct of war is represented by short periods of intensive activity punctuated by long periods of boredom and inactivity. The instruction of current affairs was not left to the whim of the commanding officer as to whether he wished his troops to be involved; he was obliged to have current affairs taught throughout his command. ABCA had its pamphlets circulated throughout the army, analysing topics and suggesting to the regimental teacher how the subject might be best presented. While the coverage was undoubtedly visionary at times, it was also radical, which accounts for its popularity among the soldiers. ABCA did disseminate some socialist propaganda because it was allowed to become the province of the enthusiastic left-winger. What they had to say in their briefing papers was also reflected and reinforced in the paper the soldiers read, namely the *Daily Mirror*. Collectively, they were potent sources to influence the course of events at war's end.

Montgomery was one of the new breed of officers who insisted the men had to know what was going on. He developed the passage of

An Army Bureau of Current Affairs course, held at the American University in Beirut in April 1943, for Non-Commissioned Officers in the Middle East. A medical officer is shown giving a lecture on plans for a post-war health service. The ABCA, which provided an opportunity for debate on current social and political affairs, was often accused of having a left-wing bias as it concentrated on progressive ideas for peace-time reconstruction.

information into an art form. He was known to stop his vehicle alongside soldiers in the road. 'Have you read a paper recently?', he would demand. On hearing the anticipated negative response, he would say, 'Here, have mine', and drive on. Meanwhile, his aide-de-camp would pass to him a replacement newspaper taken from the top of the pile he kept in the back of the vehicle. He also expected his officers to keep their men 'in the picture'. This they did because, when visiting units, one of Montgomery's tricks was to ask the soldiers what was going on. If they didn't know, then their officers were in serious trouble.

Denis Healey tells the story of an event in North Africa when Monty took the 78th Division under command. He gave one of his 'gather round me' orders, to give the new soldiers the benefit of one of his pep talks. Caught up in the rush forward and pinned up against the jeep on which Montgomery stood, was Harry Secombe. When the general had finished what he had to say, Harry Secombe, beret askew and peering through broken glasses, shouted out 'we're with you sir!' Observers could tell from Monty's look that he was not greatly encouraged by that thought. One of Monty's tricks, not appreciated by guardsmen, was his hurling of packs of cigarettes among soldiers. They treated that act with the disdain it deserved. They left the cigarettes on the ground where they fell.

The guiding lights of ABCA sought to promulgate the details of the Beveridge Report – a blueprint for a 'cradle to grave' welfare state. They saw the report not as a revolutionary proposal but rather as a step towards natural justice by rectifying the wrongs of the 1930s. Sir William Beveridge personally wrote, expressly for ABCA, a summary of his main proposals. The pamphlet was issued on 19 December 1942 and, on 21 December, was withdrawn by the War Office. The Secretary of State for War, civil servant and friend of the Prime Minister, Sir James Grigg, defended his action by saying that the discussion of such controversial proposals should not be debated in compulsory fora. By their hostility to Beveridge's report, a number of Tories in the Commons closely identified their party as opponents to change. Understandably, the Government's action, rather than stifling curiosity, caused the opposite to occur and the government found itself obliged to release copies for further discussion within the military. Of course, it was not just the military who

General Montgomery giving one of his famous 'gather round me' pep talks.

Sir William Beveridge, the liberal economist. From the time of its publication his report was a major focus of political debate, compelling the War Cabinet to appoint a Reconstruction Committee.

had been mentally stimulated. The same was true in civilian life. Queues formed outside His Majesty's Stationery Office – by no means a frequent occurrence. Over a quarter of a million copies of the full report were sold, as well as 370,000 copies of an abridged version.

The Beveridge Report had been commissioned by the coalition government as a low key feasibility study of social insurance. What the radical civil servant Sir William Beveridge gave them was a 200,000 word Declaration of Human Rights. Beveridge's critics accuse him of having had too high an opinion of himself, but he was a crusading humanitarian who put his finger exactly upon what the people wanted – cradle to grave insurance cover. Nine people out of ten believed that the Report's conclusions should be put into practice. Among the one in ten who were not immediately enthralled were those who realised that the tax burden would fall upon them in order that the costly plan might come to fruition. *The Times* thundered:

The way of the Beveridge Report is the road to moral ruin in the nation: it is the way tending to weaken still further the spirit of initiative and adventure, the stimulus of competition,

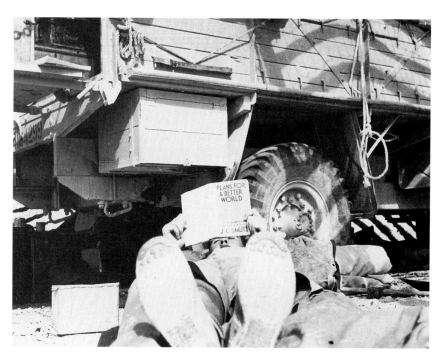

Armed conflict comprises very short periods of intensive, dangerous activity punctuated by long periods of inactivity and boredom. It was at times such as these that soldiers sought mental stimulation.

courage and self reliance. It is a blow at the heart of the nation.
It is the way of sheep.

That is not the way the disadvantaged of Britain saw the proposal.
They remembered the privations they had had to endure without
adequate welfare provision in the Great Depression of the 1930s, and
saw the Beveridge report as the beginning of the end of fearing that
no job meant living below the bread line, of homelessness and the
amelioration of the effects of becoming ill.

Churchill did not want to implement the Beveridge Report under
the auspices of the coalition government. In that respect, he passed
a considerable advantage into the hands of the Labour Party, for it
was they whom the soldiers and public believed to be most amenable
towards bringing into being the Report's recommendations.

The Labour Party were quick to
identify themselves with the
Beveridge Report. It featured
strongly as a topic in a Bristol
by-election as can be seen
from the advertisement carried
by these canvassers from
Bristol University.

However, Churchill was not opposed to the outline principles contained in Beveridge and, if the Conservatives had been elected in 1945, it seems likely that they, rather than the Labour Party, would have been identified with the Welfare State.

The euphoria of the celebration of Victory in Europe had barely subsided when thoughts turned to the General Election. People were continually reminded that the war was not over. Churchill had said in October 1944 that the war against Japan would continue for a further 18 months after victory in Europe. Plans were drawn up for the battle of Japan, equipment was repainted for the new environment but, overall, the citizens of the Home Front had become extremely parochial in their outlook. To them, Japan was a remote and distant place. For Churchill, however, there was the obligation to hit the campaign trail while still the Prime Minister of a nation at war. But, so effusive had been his reception across the country that the Labour Party seemed prepared to concede defeat before the election had been held. The *Daily Mail's* impression of Churchill's

An officer registers his vote on 5 July 1945 at a polling booth in the Royal Engineers Base Depot, near Cairo.

Winston Churchill out canvassing in his Woodford, Essex, constituency.

electioneering was 'VE Day all the way'. Churchill was unconvinced. He confided in his doctor: 'I am worried about this damned election. I have no message for them now'. After the election at home on 5 July 1945, the ballot boxes were sealed and taken into the returning officers' custody. A period of 19 days had been allowed for the Services' postal vote to be flown back from the outposts of the Empire to Great Britain. The Services' vote was most important. Over three million servicemen and women were entitled to vote and 60 per cent did (compared with 25 per cent in 1918).

The Conservatives believed that they would be returned, albeit with a reduced majority. Labour's victory, with a majority of 145 over all parties, was an emphatic victory and, despite having less than half the votes cast, was taken as a mandate for change. It was not so much a rejection of Churchill as a person but rather of the old order that he and his party represented. For him, there was sadness at home; consternation abroad. The new Labour Members of Parliament were not cloth-cap revolutionaries but representatives of the middle class who had won over the support of left-wing Conservatives and right-wing Liberals. It has been estimated that one third of the middle class voted Labour. The Tory Party, not for the first time, had lost touch with the electorate and, as a consequence, was hammered at the polls. It happened in 1832, in 1906, and it will happen again. In 1945, 'Peterborough' in *The Daily Telegraph* put forward the view that the Army Educational Corps should be given a battle honour: General Election of 1945. The view that the AEC, the system of current affairs discussions and ABCA were responsible for the Labour victory has often been challenged, particularly as the discussions were led by regimental officers.

One of the most eminent challengers was Winston Churchill himself. In an after dinner speech at Eltham Palace, then the home of the Royal Army Educational Corps (RAEC), which is what the AEC became, Lord Butler told the Corps that 'Peterborough' had claimed for it an honour to which it was not entitled – namely the Labour election victory of 1945. When the victory was announced, Churchill summoned Butler, who was then living at Eltham Palace – the home of Sir Stephen Courtauld – and where he drafted the 1944 Education Act. When Butler arrived, he was summoned into the presence and Winnie said to him: 'Rab, what have you done? It is all your fault!' Churchill was, of course, referring to Butler's association with social reform. This may well be true since the Service vote, although important, was too small to have won the election for Labour with such a landslide. Certainly the V-E Day Celebrations were as much about Beveridge and Butler as they were about the defeat of Hitler.

Churchill's public face was gracious in defeat. On 14 August, Japan surrendered. A General Election had been required by Statute in 1940 but was regularly postponed for the duration of the Churchill coalition. After their victory, the Labour Party no longer wished to continue in partnership with the Conservatives. The next day, the King opened Parliament, the first peacetime parliament since 1938. On 16 August, during the debate on the address, the new Prime Minister, Clement Attlee, paid the following tribute to Churchill:

> The surrender of Japan has brought to an end the greatest war in history, and a General Election, which was not of his seeking, has resulted in the Right Honourable Member for Woodford being on the opposition benches at a time when the fruits of his long leadership of the nation were being garnered. I think it is fitting that today I should pay a tribute to one of the

The King standing with the Labour Prime Minister, Clement Attlee, in the grounds of Buckingham Palace, 26 July 1945.

greatest architects of our victory. However we may be divided politically in this House, I believe I shall be expressing the views of the whole House in making acknowledgement here of the transcendent services rendered by the Right Honourable Gentleman to this country, to the Commonwealth and Empire, and to the world during his tenure of office as Prime Minister.

Thus the curtain fell on the collection of activities which led up to and followed on from the V-E Day celebrations. By way of a summary, there is now the introduction of three members of the House of Lords, to recount the part they played in the war and to give their views of the social and political forces which arose on either side of V-E Day. Not only did they see war service, but all three would in turn become Secretary of State for Defence. They were (alphabetically) Lord Carrington, Lord Healey and Lord Pym. It is perhaps a sign of the times that the nation's defence expertise lies in the House of Lords rather than in the House of Commons. It is not possible to think of a single Member of Parliament in the past 25 years who has had experience above the tactical level of conflict.

Lord Carrington is the only one of the trio to have been a regular officer, leaving Sandhurst in January 1939 and being commissioned into the Grenadier Guards. During the course of the prologue to war, when there 'was foreboding, tension and a sense of inevitable doom in the air', the Grenadier Guards in Wellington Barracks 'marched up and down, and were rebuked for the smallest irregularities of dress as if little else in the military sense mattered at all'. In the summer, the battalion had gone on field training for two weeks at Pirbright. There were insufficient weapons and, in order to compensate for the shortfall, the quartermaster issued broom handles. For the most part, it was ceremonial duties which held the attention of the junior officers, as had probably been the case with their fathers and grandfathers before them. The more senior the officer, the greater the latitude. For example, Lord Carrington's company commander took a house in the South of France and, between January and April 1939, simply did not appear for duty. 'Our older officers', said Lord Carrington,

> had spent too long in the deadening routine of a peacetime army which – as happened between 1919 and 1939 – is told that it has won the war to win all wars and won't take part in another conflict of any significant scale. In such an atmosphere, the small minutiae of regimental life dominate and replace all else.

The Second Grenadiers were part of 7th Guards Brigade, one of 3rd Division's brigades and earmarked to be one of the first divisions to go to France. In 1939 there was a rule that officers and men under the age of 21 were not permitted to serve abroad. Thus the 20-year old Lord Carrington did not go to war and missed Dunkirk. Instead, he commanded the demonstration platoon at the Small Arms School in Hythe. His platoon taught minor tactics by day and at night assumed its wartime role of defending three and a half miles of the coastline:

> We were confident that if the Germans landed they would suffer appallingly. I almost pitied them. I commanded forty-eight men with three light machine guns and forty-five rifles. Personally, I had a pistol.

After a period in London in 1940 suffering the Blitz, Lord Carrington rejoined his regiment in Weymouth in 1941. Among the emergency measures of 1940 aimed at defending the country from a Nazi invasion was the formation of a selected number of armoured divisions. However, the threat from Operation SEA LION had completely evaporated by the end of 1941. Yet despite shortages of first class infantry, the programme of forming armoured divisions went ahead and included a Guards Armoured Division. It was not just the question of ergonomics, of squeezing the tallest soldiers in the British army into small tank compartments, which begged questions. There was something even more fundamental. After Dunkirk, the Guards had proved themselves to be first class infantry, something they proved again in North Africa and Italy. 'This standard was achieved', said Lord Carrington,

> by a tradition of discipline and order, perhaps sometimes a touch inflexible but in infantry combat assuredly effective. The Foot Guards could be relied upon to do what they were told, and to do it conscientiously and efficiently. The tradition was less applicable to armoured warfare, or much of it. Where manoeuvre is required, so is speed and imagination and initiative. I never thought our system was perfect for breeding these qualities.

He tells the story of a sergeant-major in training on Salisbury Plain, who was constantly slow to respond on the tank radio. By chance, his tank happened to be close to the said sergeant-major's when an officer's voice addressed the sergeant-major through his earphones. 'He stood to attention and saluted before tackling the microphone.'

The war had proved to be a great leveller between regular and conscript, between officers and men and, very often, between the officers themselves. Elsewhere, the war was raging on other distant fronts but, after Dunkirk and before D-Day, the bulk of the British army was at home, training, trying not to be bored, and trying to cohere into an efficient fighting machine. Under such circumstances, living and working together at close quarters, officers and men got to know one another very well. Lord Carrington's approach was based not only upon necessary discipline, but he was also convinced of the essential need to share information by telling his subordinates what he was trying to achieve. Moreover, he exercised this policy through 'pleasantness and good manners'. He learnt that humour was one of the most important agents with which to bond a team comprising individuals of different abilities, backgrounds and expectations:

> But although the war may have been a leveller, at the best it reinforced mutual regard, made subordination human and bound a disciplined collection of men with at least some of the attributes of a loyal and devoted family.

In war there are few families closer than a tank crew – they eat, sleep, fight and sometimes die together. How extraordinarily levelling for a peer of the realm to have to fight to survive as the leader of a team of men with whom he would otherwise not have come into contact:

> They were extraordinarily nice, full of infectious humour, decent, honourable men who showed little rancour about a society in which they had drawn, to date, few prizes. So many of them had come from disadvantaged backgrounds. Two out of the four men in my tank crew had been unemployed and these were regulars who could not get work, who were hungry in civilian life; the army meant food, a roof and a job; and once they got used to it, a job in which they could take pride as compared to the dole in which there could be no pride at all. There is within my party, particularly among the group which entered the Commons in the 1980s, a view that the unemployed are ne'er do wells and workshy. That was not my experience. They do not understand what it means to be unemployed.

Ernest Bevin had gone down to the coast when embarkation was proceeding for the D-Day landings. As a soldier got into a landing craft to take him and his company over the Channel, he called out: 'Ernie, when we have done this job for you, are we going back on the dole?' Bevin wept.

What was extraordinary was the way in which the disadvantaged part of the two nations worked in such close harmony with the advantaged, to win the war. Yet for the soldiers, this was a war against two evils. Once they kicked Hitler into touch they believed that, shortly after victory had been celebrated, society's inherent unfairness would be redressed to their advantage. ABCA had been prominent in fostering these hopes. Lord Carrington, however, is not of the opinion that it was ABCA and the *Daily Mirror* which ensured that the military voted as they did in 1945. He recalls a gathering of his squadron where the discussion centred upon voting intentions.

The result of a mock 'General Election', staged by British troops in Cairo in February 1944, is displayed on a blackboard.

> Not one man intended to vote other than Labour. They wanted a change. They reckoned that a change could only be for the better, and that they had too little to cherish from life as it had been. And, as people will, they blamed the Government – the pre-war, Conservative Government. I didn't, and don't, regard that as entirely just, but I understand. For me, the result of the election was a foregone conclusion. Conventional wisdom, guided by ABCA, blamed the Government for all the pre-war ills, for unemployment and appeasement. What is strange is that people hadn't recognised the political reality.

Although Churchill's standing as a wartime leader remained high, an opinion poll in 1944 showed 62 per cent of those surveyed thought that he would be a poor peacetime leader.

The Guards Armoured Division deployed to France in June 1944 as part of an armoured corps comprising three armoured and one infantry division. The corps area, bounded by the city of Caen on one side and forests on the other, with, in the centre, random villages joined by what were often sunken lanes, was not good tank country. The fact was that General O'Connor's corps was available to be used, there was too much armour, too little infantry, and therefore it was assigned to Operation GOODWOOD. The narrow opening into the fields leading up to the Bourguebus Ridge meant that the armour could only trickle forward instead of being used *en masse* to achieve the best shock effect. The Germans up on the ridge and in the villages were totally surprised. In fact the senior German commander then present, Oberst Hans von Luck, had arrived back from Paris to witness the beginning of the deployment of the British armour below him. The limited success of GOODWOOD was very

A Sherman tank with flails goes forward past a German Mark IV tank near Cagny.

much due to this one officer's energetic efforts to cobble together a mutually supportive defence. The key weapon in the defensive battle was the 88mm Flak 18. This anti-aircraft gun was designed by a Krupp team working in Sweden to circumvent the restrictions imposed by the Treaty of Versailles. Von Luck called upon the Luftwaffe officer commanding the 88s to move their trajectory from the vertical to the horizontal and to engage the tanks to his front.

'This', said the Luftwaffe officer, 'is a Luftwaffe unit whose role is to engage aircraft, not tanks'. Thereupon von Luck drew his Luger and, pointing it at the airforce officer's skull, said evenly: 'Do you wish to be recommended for a high decoration, or dead?' At which point the 88s, in conjunction with those tanks which had survived the preliminary air bombardment, engaged the British armour in such a manner as to resemble a turkey shoot.

For Lord Carrington, under fire for the first time and following behind 11th Armoured Division, the picture ahead of him was not at all encouraging. Up on the skyline he could see a large number of the lead division's tanks ablaze. Very soon the Guards Armoured Division was also to lose over 20 tanks in the first few hours. 'A mass of tanks', said Lord Carrington,

> is an excellent force with which to exploit a tactical victory, but to achieve that victory needed the co-ordination of a limited number of tanks with a large number of skilled infantry and

mortars – in order to deal with the scatter of German strong-points which so successfully held up the armoured advance.

4 Company, 1st Battalion the Welsh Guards attacking the enemy from a concealed position near Cagny.

The generals were quick to learn the lesson of the different nature of warfare in western Europe as opposed to North Africa. First Guards Armoured Division was hurriedly reorganised in order to provide squadron-company groups comprising a mix of armour and infantry.

After a short, recuperative period, the Guards Armoured Division advanced against only light opposition through northern France and into Brussels. The next operation – MARKET GARDEN – was an altogether different proposition, advancing along a road in Holland to link up with the paratroopers who had been dropped in and around Arnhem to secure the Rhine bridge, but who were being systematically destroyed by the Germans. The British First Airborne Division had been dropped in an area where the best panzer divisions

Operation MARKET GARDEN. Parachutists of the British First Airborne Division fighting off German Panzers, waiting for relief that never came. Arnhem was rightly judged a 'bridge too far'.

in the German army were refitting. On 5 September, Bletchley Park decoded a message and sent it to Montgomery's Headquarters.

> For rest and refit of panzer formations, Heeresgruppe (army group) Baker ordered afternoon fourth (4 September) to remain in operation with battleworthy elements: two panzer, one arc six panzer, nine SS and one nought (ten) SS panzer divisions, elements not operating to be transferred by AOK five for rest and refit in area Venlo-Arnhem-Hertogenbosch.

This vital warning, which was supported by Dutch resistance reports of a heavy concentration of German armour in the Arnhem area, was not acted upon. Intelligence by itself is insufficient. It requires interpretation and decisions made as to the appropriate action. In this case, the intelligence was either overlooked or deliberately ignored.

Resupply aircraft did their best to support the paras until the juncture could be made with the relief force. For the Guards, who were so near and yet so far, the sight of the heroic air activity proved immensely moving. 'Many were brought down. I thought the pilots wonderfully brave, such easy targets, such devoted men.' The story is history – Arnhem did prove to be a bridge too far, but the Guards captured the bridge at Nijmegen, where Lord Carrington won a Military Cross. Winter was spent in Holland. In early 1945 the Rhine was crossed and, when the ceasefire was signed, the Guards

Armoured Division was at Cuxhaven in northern Germany. In the style and manner of the Brigade of Guards, their massed bands were flown over to Germany to take part in a huge parade held at Rothenburg airfield on 9 June 1945. General Montgomery took the salute and, at the end, the Guards reverted to being foot soldiers and looked forward to the benefits of their victory and demobilisation. 'I do not remember much at all about the V-E Day celebrations', admitted Lord Carrington.

> I do remember, two weeks before, not wanting to get hurt as it was perfectly clear the war was ending. Perhaps that's why V-E Day was such an anti-climax, it didn't mean much at all, the war just stopped.

Denis Healey's war experience provides a useful contrast to the experience of Lord Carrington. When war was declared he came forward to join the Royal Artillery, despite being a member of the British Communist Party. He said that people joined the Communist Party because they were against Hitler. He waited for the call to arms but instead was encouraged to return to Balliol College, Oxford, which he would leave with a Double First. At the age of 23 and after a brief period serving in Keighley's Home Guard, he was summoned to report to Uniacke Barracks near Harrogate. 'Unfashionable though it is to admit it, I enjoyed my five years in the wartime army. It was a life very different from anything I had known, or expected.'

The medical inspection at the Depot revealed a rupture which, after due attention, resulted in a posting near to his place of birth at Woolwich. Passing through London at the end of 1940 had a profound impact. The tunnels of the Underground system were not just the places of the transitee but of women and children going below ground to escape the worst effects of the Blitz. Woolwich was in a sorry looking state. 'Like Dante's Purgatory, with more than a smattering of the Inferno.' The monotony of routine preyed upon bored soldiers in grubby barracks. Grossly under-employed, they were nevertheless confined to barracks for all but one hour before blackout. They got by. Just how, was revealed when the barracks was hit by a stick of bombs. The hurriedly assembled parade, drawn up to identify casualties, revealed there to be several hundred unaccounted for. They were not injured or killed, but cuddled up in the bosom of female friends not far distant from the camp.

The bombers came up the Thames after sunset, introduced by the wailing of sirens and sought out by searchlights like fiery fingers stabbing deep into the dark. In response to the detection of an intruder locked in intersecting beams of light, the big guns to the rear of the barracks opened up with a crescendo of pulsating noise which shook the buildings to their foundations.

> One evening about forty of us were sitting in the canteen when suddenly, as if at a signal, everyone flopped to the floor. The noise of falling chairs and breaking cups made me think a bomb had fallen just outside. The room looked like a Muslim prayer meeting – a mass of khaki backsides raised to heaven and heads hidden under marble tables. Then, suddenly, everyone rose again to continue talking, as if nothing had happened. In fact nothing had happened; it was a good example of the psychology of crowds.

Early in 1941, Denis Healey was posted to Swindon Railway Station to replace a drunken bombardier. His place of duty was the Railway Traffic Office, a small establishment which, after the war, survived over 40 years of swingeing defence cuts, presumably because it was overlooked. Swindon proved to be an important posting, for it introduced Denis Healey to the world of Movement Control – not a gunner activity, but one in the gift of the Royal Engineers. What was required of him was to register those getting off trains and those getting on trains. This proved to be enormously difficult. Not only had he not fully recovered from his operation, but there were also six platforms, at their busiest during blackout. He solved his problem by creative accounting.

> I made up the number getting off and on again, made an informed guess of the number getting on, and asked the ticket collector for the numbers getting off. After a few weeks I discovered he was making up his figures as well. This gave me a life-long scepticism about the reliability of statistics, which served me well when I became Chancellor of the Exchequer. It

also taught me never to take for granted any information I was given, unless I was able to check it from another source at least once.

After Swindon came a training course at Derby, with whistle-stop postings as the Rail Traffic Officer in Hull, Halifax, York, Leeds and Sheffield. By now, something more challenging was needed so, in the summer of 1942, Denis Healey volunteered for training in combined operations, with a view to becoming an Assistant Military Landing Officer in a Beach Group. The disaster at Dieppe revealed the need for original work and understanding in this particular, important area. The accumulating experience and practical lessons learnt thus far were to serve Denis Healey well in his future political life.

Boring, mechanical and irrelevant as a lot of my training was, I learned much of permanent value. The basic drill, which seemed so senseless at the time, enabled me to carry out standard movements without thinking, thus freeing my mind for more important tasks in a crisis. Army Staff training helped me to analyse problems systematically and to prescribe the necessary action clearly. General Urquhart's operational order for the landing in Calabria only ran to three pages. *(This is Major General R E Urquhart, who later won fame at Arnhem – RC.)* Business schools are supposed to perform a similar role for industry. For someone like me, who had spent his previous life at school and university, the army was a school in practical reality. After loading tanks on to railway flats during the blackout, in a blizzard, on the moors above Penistone, I will never again go to a job without a pencil and paper.

For me as an individualist intellectual, however, the most valuable legacy of war service was the knowledge that I depended on other people, and that other people depended on me. It was this knowledge which created the sense of comradeship so characteristic of wartime and so lacking in peace. Combined operations taught me another lesson – that every group in society has its own special contribution to make through its own special knowledge and experience. The average soldier took the navy and airforce for granted; they provided him with protection at sea and in the sky, but he did not realise that their job was as complicated and as dangerous as his own. It came at first as a surprise to me to realise that the navy's job in getting the troops on to a beach was quite as complicated as mine in getting them across and off it.

Finally, no one can go through a war without accepting the importance of planning. Individual initiative and personal bravery have, of course, a vital role. But without the most careful planning, involving consultation with all the interests concerned, no operation has a chance of success. Needless to say, planning can often go badly wrong, as I was to discover in some of the operations I helped to organise. In war, even more than in peace, it is impossible to know all the relevant facts when you make the plan – and you are working against an enemy whose own plans are designed to frustrate yours. But to rule out the desirability or even possibility of planning in principle, as some politicians do, is to accept an intolerable handicap and to betray those for whom you are responsible. No industrial manager would accept such a handicap; yet many governments do. Oddly enough, the magic of the market place on which they prefer to rely, usually depends on the unco-ordinated plans of innumerable private groups.

Denis Healey did find the Services very class-structured, but no more so than industry. He observed that officers acted differently, wore different clothes and ate different food. As the conscripts percolated through, those with ability received rapid promotion, particularly in the newly-established disciplines such as combined operations and specialist intelligence. He found the regular officers to be of varied quality, but those with limitations had been filtered out prior to the landings in North Africa, due to the fiasco with the BEF in France. The promotion of officers on the basis of ability and suitability was not universally welcomed, as was apparent from this extract of a letter which appeared in *The Times* in January 1941:

Never has the old school tie and the best it stands for been more justified than it is today. Our new armies are being officered by classes of society who are new to the job. The middle, lower middle and working classes are now receiving the King's Commission. These classes, unlike the old aristocratic and feudal (almost) classes who led the old Army, had never their people to consider. They have never had anyone to think of but themselves. This aspect of life is particularly new to them, and they have very largely fallen down on it in their capacity as Army officers.

The War Office's manning department was one of that organisation's strengths. The selection and promotion system was intelligently conducted. The good were promoted early, as indeed did the able men from the ranks progress according to their ability. Politically, ABCA and the *Daily Mirror* did not perform a decisive role in socialising the military, although the war did awaken people to the fact that there was such a thing as Socialism. Those who went into politics after the war, did so out of a sense of developing society. This moral dimension ran right through the army's rank structure. 'By 1943', said Denis Healey, 'you could not take it for granted that a General was not a Labour supporter'.

On 13 April 1943, Denis Healey left Glasgow to join the war. He did not know where he was bound until past Gibraltar. After 10 days

Major Denis Healey in Italy.
Source: Private.

at sea he disembarked at Algiers, always behind the action as the advance continued towards the Bay of Tunis with the intention of eventually landing in Sicily.

Controversy surrounded the Allied decision to invade Sicily and Italy in 1943. President Roosevelt urged that the invasion of Europe through Normandy should proceed without further diversions. This proposal had not impressed Stalin who preferred his Allies to conduct operations most likely to draw German forces away from the Russian front. The Russian position encouraged Churchill to recommend a rapid advance up 'the soft underbelly' of Europe. He argued that such a campaign would satisfy Russian demands, hold the attention of Germans and Italians deployed in that theatre, and consolidate the Allied position in the Mediterranean. With the focus of attention on the principal invasion of Europe, the Italian campaign was destined to become a sideshow. One ill-informed female commentator referred to the Allied troops fighting in Italy as 'D-Day dodgers'. Soft underbelly it was not: 'more', according to Denis Healey, 'a bristling spine'.

Denis Healey's switching from the Salerno landing to take the appointment of beachmaster for a landing at Calabria, designed to cut off the Germans retreating from Sicily, proved to be opportune. The officer selected in his place was killed only hours after landing at Salerno. The Calabria assault troops set sail on 7 September 1943. Whilst preparing, the word was passed that Italy had surrendered on 3 September. That was cold comfort, for this particular assault was against Germans, not Italians. Moreover, German contingency plans resulted in their reinforcement of Italy. A description of the military disaster which followed at Calabria can be found in most good history books. The brigade to which Denis Healey was attached withdrew after the landing in order to join D-Day preparations, the 200 casualties were evacuated to Sicily and the beachmaster acquired an amphibious jeep, 'like a bathtub on wheels, which I managed to keep through most of the campaign in Italy'.

Denis Healey was beachmaster for the Allied landing on 22 January 1944 at Anzio. This landing on the west coast of Italy, behind the Gustav Line and Monte Cassino, was designed to break the stalemate to the south. Arguments still persist as to the manner in which the landing was conducted but, having achieved initial

The beach in Anzio, Italy.

surprise, the attackers lost the initiative, barely managing to hold on until Monte Cassino fell in May 1944. The road to Rome was open, and then came the demoralising discovery that the Gothic Line to the north was going to test the Allies as much as the Gustav Line had done. The fighting lasted from 25 August 1944 to 2 May 1945, when the Germans surrendered. 'V-E Day did not mean much to us at the time', admitted Healey, 'since we thought we might have to go to the Far East from Europe; so V-J Day was more important since it marked the end of the whole war'.

Meanwhile Healey, who had been selected to fight the safe Conservative seat of Pudsey and Otley, was given three months' leave of absence from duty in Italy to fight the seat. He arrived in England in time to attend the Labour Party Conference held at Blackpool on 21 May 1945. With his attention held by the war, Denis Healey had little idea of what was going on politically in Great Britain. He had only the vaguest thoughts of the Beveridge Plan and the Labour Party but, what he did know was that he wanted a change for the better, and he knew that could only be achieved through a change of Government:

> The Conservatives were discredited by memories of the Great Slump and of appeasement. Their main asset, Winston

Churchill, threw away his potential advantages by accusing Labour of wanting to introduce a Gestapo into Britain; he was handicapped by his obvious inability to understand the men and women he had led in war. Do you know, in one broadcast he addressed the British people as, 'you who are listening to me in your cottages'.

Major Healey's vituperative speech at the Blackpool Conference was not made of the stuff likely to win over the middle classes but, rather, good old table-thumping socialism:

The upper classes in every country are selfish, depraved, dissolute and decadent. The struggle for socialism in Europe . . . has been hard, cruel, merciless and bloody. The penalty for participation in the liberation movement has been death of oneself, if caught, and, if not caught oneself, the burning of one's home and the death by torture of one's family . . . Remember that one of the prices paid for our survival during the last five years has been the death by bombardment of countless thousands of innocent European men and women.

A preponderance of artillery was a principal reason for the British success at El Alamein.

He cut the Conservative majority in Pudsey and Otley from 10,000 to 1,651 and, presumably on the basis of his rousing speech, was offered, and accepted, the post of International Secretary of the Labour Party.

Sherman tanks. Their 75 mm. gun turret and high speed surprised the enemy and turned the tide in armoured warfare.

The turning of the corner, away from doubt and defeat, had been Montgomery's victory over the Africa Corps at El Alamein, October–November 1942. The principal reason why Montgomery succeeded while those before him failed was because he insisted upon being given the resources he deemed necessary to do the job. It was a major strategic decision at the height of the Atlantic war to send 25,000 reinforcements out to the 8th Army. Among that number was one 20-year-old Francis Pym. The future Lord Pym was a troop leader in the 9th Lancers. When the famous, massive artillery barrage opened up against the Axis positions, they were heavily outnumbered in the air and on land, and their supply route across the Mediterranean had also been severely interdicted. The Axis forces stood up against the pounding for 14 days until, on 4 November, the line broke and they were forced to withdraw westward. Before the battle ended, on 8 November 1942, the advance troops of Operation TORCH had landed in Morocco and Algeria. The subsequent defeat of the Axis powers in North Africa, after a

Francis Pym as a subaltern in the 9th Lancers. (Private)

further series of very hard fought battles such as that of the Mareth Line, gave the people at home something to cheer about after a string of defeats. The Battle of Alamein was truly the first, dim light at the end of what was still a long tunnel.

Francis Pym described Montgomery as the new broom. He was fortunate to find the 8th Army equipped for the first time with weapons equivalent to those possessed by the Africa Corps. The 9th Lancers had gone into France in 1939 with little ammunition, which soon ran out, and they were left with just smoke. They were extraordinarily lucky to escape. The Crusader's armour was as thin as butter. Only when the Shermans came on stream in quantities did the tide begin to turn. Francis Pym also confirmed that Montgomery insisted upon every man knowing what was happening. Lieutenant Pym met Montgomery for the first time one week into the Battle of Alamein when Monty awarded an instant Military Medal to a corporal in the 9th Lancers, a poacher by profession, who had knocked out the most enemy tanks. He impressed the young subaltern by his assuredness, confidence and certainty of victory.

After that first success, Francis Pym recounted how Monty developed a capacity to irritate those with whom he worked: 'He got too big for his boots'. That seems to have been a common opinion. Although Lord Carrington credits Montgomery with instilling into the British Army a long overdue professionalism, he also found the man to be bumptious and conceited: 'I am not a military historian but I have a strong impression that Monty's generalship was on occasions described in over-generous terms by Monty'. Denis Healey was not a fan. He was among a large number of the 1st Army drawn up to listen to one of Monty's inspirational addresses:

> He did not impress me with his sharp, ferret-like face and pale grey-green eyes, wearing his vanity like a foulard. When he told the veterans of 78 Division, who had almost taken Tunis within three days of landing at Algiers, that they should feel proud to be joining the 8th Army, the temperature dropped below freezing in a second.

The 9th Lancers moved into Italy where the Germans' fighting qualities impressed Francis Pym:

. . . Montgomery in Sicily. In Lord Pym's opinion 'He got too big for his boots.' Lord Carrington believes his '. . . generalship was on occasions described in over-generous terms by Monty.' Lord Healey was not impressed '. . . with his sharp, ferret-like face and pale grey-green eyes, wearing his vanity like a foulard.'

They were very tough and had great resolution and high morale. They defended the Gothic line with great tenacity: it took from 5 September to Christmas 1944 to break right through.

We operated in close support of infantry battalions and were attacking the enemy throughout that period virtually without a break. We advanced thirty miles as the crow flies in that time and assisted in forcing crossings over five rivers. While casualties were fairly light they happened continuously.

In January and February 1945 we became infantry because the terrain and the wet weather made the going difficult for tanks. In this unaccustomed role we lost four men killed and thirty-three were wounded.

The final phase of the war for us began in March when we started operating with an infantry battalion mounted in tracked vehicles. Together we operated extremely effectively during four attacks in the Po valley with low casualties – and against Germans far weaker and less dangerous than those up in the Gothic line.

Francis Pym was Adjutant of his regiment from March 1943 until the end of the war and won the Military Cross in Italy. In the few pauses there were in that gruelling campaign, there was of course ABCA to occupy minds which might otherwise have been bored.

ABCA was not spreading socialist doctrine offensively, it's just that there was no counter view available. It was only those inclined to support the Labour Party who were engaging in this activity and the soldiers found corroboration in the papers they read – *Picture Post*, *The Daily Mirror* and *The Daily Herald*.

I can remember the moment peace was declared in Europe. We were in a village in northern Italy, fifty miles from Venice. The priest ran through the street to ring the church bells. When you're in a regiment of tanks you have nothing with which to celebrate other than to reflect, thank God that's over. I recall the sheer relief and enjoyment, and the realisation that I had survived.

My father was then Member of Parliament for Monmouth and a Whip in both the wartime coalition government and the caretaker government. He fought the 1945 election but died in the period between the closing of the poll and the declaration: he was re-elected posthumously and the future Lord Thorneycroft was then elected in his place.

To my mind the most important post-war decision was the creation of the United Nations, born out of an understanding that the world could never again have another war such as that just experienced and must have an effective international mechanism to maintain peace. By the same token, the electorate was confident enough to want something different. A regiment is dedicated to winning the next battle but, when the political options became available, the soldiers were no different from anyone else: they wanted change and went for what they thought would be the most attractive future.

So, from the activities of ABCA, Churchill's election defeat and the visions of three soldiers eventually to become Secretaries of State for Defence and members of the House of Lords, it can be seen that V-E Day was a complex celebration – exultant, but not vengeful, restrained rather than drunken, full of memory and thanksgiving, sadness and joy, the end of war and the beginning of peace, but perhaps above all, a forward-looking and visionary moment in time when men and women having crested the hill stood and looked with hand above eyes into the dawn.

To what extent did that dawn herald the arrival of a better, fairer, juster world – the world that Carrington, Healey and Pym hoped for, as well as J B Priestley, Beveridge, Butler, Atlee, Bevin and all the men and women remembered in this book?

It is not the purpose of this book to answer that question, only to ask it, and to suggest that in this 50th V-E Day anniversary year, some time and thought could, with profit, be given by its readers to formulate an answer – an answer that will incorporate the Iron Curtain and Soviet repression, Czechoslovakia 1948, Hungary and Suez 1956, post-Cold War Yugoslavia, the decline of British wealth and power, the failures of the Welfare State, as well as the elimination of Fascism and the creation of the United Nations. Other thoughts would include the more equitable distribution of wealth in society, the creation of free medical services and free secondary education for all, old age pensions, better housing, and all the many social and economic improvements that distinguish the 1930s from the 1990s in these once so beleaguered and – in 1945 – so triumphant islands. It seems that the real importance of the Celebration of Victory on 8 May 1945 is that it was a deciding moment in history which delivered what 1918-19 had only promised.